MEMORIES OF THE

Lancashire Fishing Industry

Ron Freethy

D1347283

COUNTRYSIDE BOOKS
NEWBURY BERKSHIRE

First published 2010
© Ron Freethy 2010

COUNTRYSIDE BOOKS
3 Catherine Road
Newbury, Berkshire

To view our complete range of books,
please visit us at
www.countrysidebooks.co.uk

ISBN 978 1 84674 212 5

De   gn

Produc   ading
Typeset by CJWT Solutions, St Helens
Printed by Information Press, Oxford

Contents

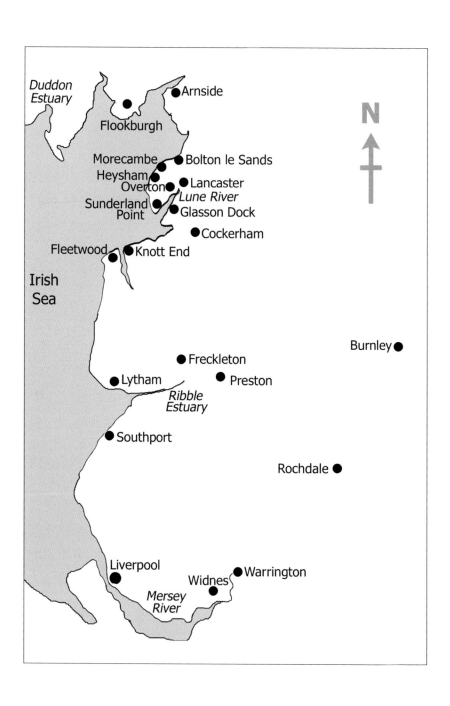

Introduction

When I first set out to record the memories of those involved in the Lancashire fishing industry, I thought I would be discovering Fleetwood in the days when it was a major deep sea fishing port and perhaps be in search of the world's first fish and chip shop! I soon found, however, that there were fishing families still around today in the county whose roots were so deep that they could probably be traced back to the days before written records began.

I was surprised and delighted to discover how many of these old and proud fishing families still exist and how many are still involved in fishing. This book is really their story. I'm sure that somewhere in their make up there must be a gene labelled 'fishing', and we all have some elements of seawater in our blood! We all – or most of us – eat fish and other gifts from the sea. The Lancashire fishing industry is therefore very much part of our country's heritage.

So would I find people whose memories go back to the early days of Lancashire's fishing industry? I need not have worried! Memories and photographs came pouring in by every post and the local museums at Fleetwood and Lancaster had massive archives to which they allowed me free access and for which I am very grateful. In the chapters that follow I will set out to discover the history of fishing from its origins around the shallow waters of the Lancashire coast to the deepest, coldest waters of the dangerous Arctic Ocean.

Ron Freethy

Acknowledgements

Authors of books such as this need a lot of help: I asked for assistance and I was not disappointed. Those who helped me are mentioned in the text but some individuals deserve a special acknowledgement.

As I started to think about this book I had the pleasure of meeting Joyce Openshaw, whose father established the *Iago* trawler fleet based in Fleetwood. I also had meetings with Lionel Marr, whose family were prominent trawler owners in Hull and especially in Fleetwood. Both these people still have a love for the history of the Lancashire fishing industry and like me are sad at the demise of our trawler fleets.

Whilst aboard the restored Marr trawler, the *Jacinta*, I met the crew and their affection for the vessel was very obvious. I also met David Pearce who was once the Dock Correspondent at Fleetwood when that port was busy.

The staff of the Fleetwood Maritime Museum, led by Lynn Asgar and Dick Gillingham, were friendly and helpful and gave me full access to the substantial archives. I had the same help from the Maritime Museum in Lancaster where the curator Michelle Cooper provided me with invaluable information. At both these museums I was introduced to volunteer staff who had been involved with fishing all of their lives and their memories are recorded throughout this present volume.

There must also be a dedication in this book and this should be to remember those fishermen who died at sea in both war and peace. The exhibits at the Fleetwood Museum give thanks for the sacrifices made and I can but add these few inadequate words to their memory. I owe a debt of gratitude also to Sam Barton, whose father was lost on the *Evelyn Rose* on New Year's Eve 1954;

Lionel Marr (left) and the author aboard the Jacinta, *discussing the history of the Marr trawler fleet.*

Sam is still trying to locate his body and bring him home to rest in peace.

Those readers who wish to enjoy visual material on the Internet may like to refer to the following websites:

The Bosun's Watch – www.fleetwood-trawlers.info

Fleetwood Online Archive of Trawlers –
    http://float-trawlers.lancashire.gov.uk

Finally, the research notes for this volume will be passed on to the Fleetwood Museum and this means that those who recall their own memories as they read this book may like to contribute to the archive. They can enjoy talking to the staff there, who welcome people with a similar history and are happy to share a 'brew' with them.

Chapter 1

The Bounty of the Sea

Apart from fish there are many other tasty morsels to be enjoyed from catches around our coastline, including cockles, mussels, prawns and shrimps. Most restaurants in the county proudly present Morecambe Bay shrimps as a starter and many town markets and fishmongers sell 'sea fresh cockles and mussels'.

The Cocklers and Musselers

As a young lad during the Second World War, I went cockling with my uncles and from an early age I knew the rules. You waited on a sandy shore for the tide to ebb. You then followed the retreating water and looked at your watch to know that you had at least four hours of safe fishing. When your sack was full – which was soon on a good day – it was off home where the cockles were washed, boiled, soaked in vinegar and then were ready to be eaten.

Most of those who gather cockles have enjoyed this skill for generations. There were no especial dangers in the old days when cockling families took what they needed for their own use, with some to sell or barter. Moving on from one good area to another, they were not exploiters but farmers.

In some areas cockling became commercial early on and the sacks were placed in handcarts. Once the railways arrived, from the 1850s onwards, there was a ready market in the industrial cotton towns. The train would be met by salesmen, who carried baskets of seafood and toured the local pubs.

One important commercial cockling area was on the Horsebank, off the coast of Lytham. I spoke to 91-year-old John Hutton whose late wife's family made a living from cockling and knew the history of the area

'well enough to keep me safe. She told me that there had once been a green pasture used by cattle until the 1590s. It then seems that there were current changes out at sea and sand banks developed and gradually deepened. These rich sands were washed by the ebb and flow of the tide and cockles thrived there. I still have a photograph taken round about 1870 which shows women cocklers hard at work and the carts ready to be loaded and taken to the station. I'll tell you what was really strange. My wife gave me cockles, which she hated but I loved. Her mother didn't eat cockles much either because they were almost brought up on a diet of cockles and bread when everybody was hard up. We don't know how lucky we are today.'

When I set out to research the history of Lancashire's fishing industry I had not expected to discover just how important the so-called shell-fishing industry once was. I was also surprised to find just how many of these traditional techniques have survived and what vivid memories there were to recall. In the course of my life as an ecologist and working for the BBC and Granada television I have had the privilege of interviewing many Lancashire people who made their living from the sea. One of the most fascinating people I met was Cedric Robinson, who has been a Morecambe Bay guide for many years and leads the cross-bay walks.

Cedric has been an expert cockler around the Flookburgh area all his life and knows the twin dangers of over-fishing, or should it be 'over-cockling', and over-confidence:

> 'We knew the tides very well and this is why my father and I survived. We could follow the ebb tide with our horse and cart often up to eight miles on the sands and in all weathers. We know where the cockle beds are and after we have harvested them we leave them alone for two years so that the population can increase and grow.'

This is what went so badly wrong in the case of the 2004 cockling disaster in Morecambe Bay, which many of us knew was just waiting to happen. So keen were some businessmen to make maximum profits that they paid too little attention to tidal conditions or indeed to the living conditions of the Chinese workers brought in illegally to work for a mere pittance. In fact, a local newspaper mindful of the situation had asked me to cover events just days before the accident happened. The disaster brought cockling into focus and it is now closely regulated. In the case of Cedric Robinson and his colleagues no legislation would have been needed because nobody knew the conditions better than they did. All this is clearly detailed in Cedric's book, *Sand Pilot of Morecambe Bay*.

Cedric went on:

> 'To harvest our cockles we use two things, a "jumbo" and a "craam". The jumbo is a wooden board with long handles. This you rock to and fro and this creates a sort of suction which sucks the cockles to the surface. You then use the craam which is a sort of large fork with knobs on. It has a long wooden handle with three metal prongs at the end. A skilled cockler can flick the cockles into a basket and then on to a trailer on a tractor. You can't just rely on cockles to make a living. I also catch flounders, a flat fish which we call flukes and I go shrimping.'

From the age of eight on the Duddon estuary I knew, along with the rest of my friends, to appreciate the danger of the tide. I learnt how to catch flounders, also known as flukes or dabs, and had two methods of catching them which had been passed on from one generation to another. If you had the time and the energy, you laid out a line of poles and between them was a string from which dangled hooks, which were baited. You baited before the tide came in and collected the caught fish at the ebb of the tide before the seagulls tried to feast upon them.

Another traditional method of catching dabs has still survived in the coastal villages and this is 'trampling'. Many small flukes known as dabs bury themselves in the sand beneath pools left by the ebbing tide. The method is to stroll around barefoot and use your toes to feel the wriggling fish beneath your feet. You then dig with your hands until the fish emerges. The best fluking time is from October to just after Christmas so all who go trampling are used to having very cold feet. It is worth it, however, because the little dabs are very sweet tasting – they can still be obtained in season from local supermarkets.

Because its coastline is more sandy than rocky, Lancashire is more of a cockling county than it is mussel-bound. There are, however, some rocky areas, especially around Morecambe and Heysham, where the mussels were commercially exploited. Many people are still worried about being poisoned by mussels but the French do not worry about this and neither should we if we take the essential precautions. Mussels, like cockles, are filter feeders and therefore can pick up 'unwanted items'. All you have to do is to place the shellfish in fresh water for 24 hours and the impurities are filtered out.

Nellie Carbis, who lived near Preston and was in her nineties when I interviewed her for a radio programme, told me:

'I had my own little garden and grew my own onions. One of my nephews made his living from fishing and musseling and always called in on me with a dish of mussels from the rocks below Heysham Head. I boiled these with onion but

Morecambe Bay musselers carrying out their back-breaking work in the 1920s.

I added my own bits and bats to avoid being totally French. I added carrot and turnip to make a stew and served it with home-made bread.'

Two days later I collected mussels from the same place and Nellie produced a wonderful Lancashire onion and mussel stew which my wife and I still make and tuck into to the present day.

I enjoy cockling but those who do this for a living today have my sympathy. Imagine a windy day with sleet blowing in your face and standing in ice-cold seawater puddles, operating a craam and carrying a heavy, wet sack. All fisherfolk earn every penny, and where would we be without them?

The shrimpers

As part of a BBC series I was recording for Radio Lancashire called 'Lancashire at Work', I interviewed Jean Rimmer in the company of the late Benita Moore. Jean is far better known as the 'shrimp lady'. She stood the markets in several Lancashire towns and she lived at Tarleton near Southport. Her family had been shrimping and fisherfolk for generations. Jean's husband caught the shrimps and Jean cooked them and prepared them for market.

She combined the selling of shrimps with a mix of seasonal home-grown tomatoes and watercress, plus crispy lettuce. There wasn't a plastic wrapping in sight and you did not need a Union Jack stamped on it to prove that it was home-grown. You could smell the freshness and had to brush off the sand and soil before enjoying it. What about a meal of shrimps and new potatoes? Lovely!

Jean Rimmer, 'The Shrimp Lady'.

The old timers knew how to catch shrimps in numbers but did not have the detailed ecological knowledge we have at our disposal today. How many people, for example, know the difference between a shrimp and a prawn?

The common prawn (*Leander serratus*) grows up to 2½ inches in length and is found in deepish water around the seas of Britain but moves into shallow water to spawn. The common shrimp (*Crangon vulgaris*) is slightly smaller but is confined to shallower waters and hence this is the species fished for along the Lancashire coast.

There are several physical differences between prawns and shrimps. Both species belong to a class of crustaceans called decapods which means, like crabs and lobsters, that they have five pairs of legs. In the case of the prawn there is a powerful set

Shrimpers at work circa 1890.

of large pincers on the second pair of walking legs but in shrimps these larger pincers are on the first pair of walking legs. Compared to the prawn, the body of the shrimp is much flatter. There is a beak-like plate on the back of shrimps and prawns but in the prawn this structure, which is called the 'rostrum', has a long serrated edge and protrudes beyond the prominent eyes. The rostrum of the shrimp does not protrude so far and is smooth.

There is also, as mentioned, a distinct habitat preference between the two. For most of the year prawns occur in deeper areas of the sea and, in consequence, they are caught from vessels. Shrimps on the other hand occur in tidal areas and have been caught in nets either operated by hand or trailed behind a horse or tractor. This method is therefore a tidal occupation and, just like cockling, needs to be done by careful reference to tidal movements and the catch should be collected on the ebb.

Shrimping went on on both sides of the Ribble estuary. When the menfolk went fishing and prawning, the women and children followed the ebb of the tide, scooped up shrimps in huge nets and put these into wicker baskets which were carried across the shoulders of strong young boys.

There developed a spin-off trade of weaving willow baskets, especially around Mawdesley, which is just inland from Southport, and fisherfolk provided a ready market – providing the price was right. When I was a child, always fascinated by the countryside, I spent time in the company of Will Everitt. He was a basketmaker who showed me how the willow wands were magically woven. What surprised me was the sheer strength and skill of his fingers, and Will worked until he was in his nineties.

Fisherfolk needed not only strength of fingers, but strength of arm, shoulder and mind as they pitted their wits against the might of the sea. In the case of Barbara Woodhouse, her family fortunes were very much based on shrimping. I found Barbara at the Lancaster Maritime Museum where she has worked for more than 30 years. Barbara is an ideal guide because she has known about shrimping from the day she was born:

'My father was Dick Woodhouse who worked out of Morecambe as a shrimper but he also made some of his living from running pleasure boats out from Morecambe Pier. He was also the much respected coxswain of the Morecambe Lifeboat.'

At the peak of the prawning era from the 1850s, many shipyards, especially Crossfields at Arnside, were busy building and repairing purpose-built vessels called 'nobbies' and these Barbara Woodhouse still speaks of with great affection. There is a delightful little booklet on sale in the Lancaster Maritime Museum called *Potted Tales* by David Stocker, which consists of transcriptions of interviews given by Morecambe's fisherfolk.

Morecambe's industry, as opposed to families only intent upon feeding their own families, dates from around 1750. The name Morecambe did not even exist at this time and actually evolved because of the developing tourist industry. Prior to that, the fishing was concentrated around the little hamlet of Poulton-le-Sands. The nucleus of this settlement can still be recognised today.

Fisherfolk tended to have large families, with the men doing the fishing and the girls carrying out the processing. When the railway arrived in 1847 the harvest from the sea could be transported very quickly to reach rich and poor alike. Victorian gentry and the newly affluent mill-owners loved their afternoon tea of potted shrimps served with bread and butter. The shrimpers of the Bay had a second and just as lucrative a market in industrial Lancashire with, as already briefly mentioned, the seafood and muffin sellers touring the local pubs. I remember Saturday nights at my Burnley local in the 1970s looking forward to my pint, plus a muffin packed with potted shrimps.

I spoke at length to Barbara Woodhouse who clearly remembers that:

'Shrimps were our family business. Dad went out in his nobby and as soon as he returned with his catch we womenfolk including the children set about "picking" the shrimps, which was our way of topping and tailing them. Firstly, though, we had to cook them by briefly boiling them. We used boiled seawater with the shrimps placed in gauze bags. We did all this in our own kitchen and we placed the shrimps in pots and then poured melted butter on them. Once the pot was full we pressed the shrimps down with a lid made of grease-proofed paper. I still think that our shrimps were the best and they are still in my view the best thing on the planet. The reason that our shrimps tasted different was that we boiled them in salt water whilst most other villagers boiled them in fresh water.

'There were times when Dad realised that he had a huge catch and there might be a problem getting the shrimps ready for the Lancashire and Yorkshire bound trains. Each nobby had a large cauldron beneath which was a coal-fired boiler. Some prawns were therefore ready for buttering by the time our handcart full of the catch reached our cottage. The idea then was that Dad went to bed and the family

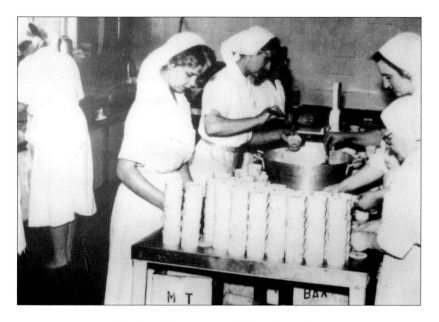

Potting shrimps is very labour-intensive.

prepared the shrimps. Dad later got up and took the shrimps to the station.'

Although Morecambe was the busiest of the fishing villages there were also family-owned nobbies operating all around the Bay, especially at Sunderland Point, Overton, Glasson Dock and Flookburgh.

There was still a strange language used by fisherfolk, who measured their shrimps not by weight but by volume and their catch was measured in 'mollinges'. There were three mollinges to one stone (14 pounds). It is still a treat to find some local pubs around the Bay selling a pint of prawns. Although prawning families are now something of a rarity it is worthwhile visiting Ray Edmonson's fish shop on Yorkshire Street in Morecambe and Barbara Woodhouse proudly told me that her father taught Ray how to fish. She also recalled:

Cockle 'fishing' at Pilling Beach at low tide. This photograph was taken just days before the Chinese cockling disaster in 2004.

'Shrimpers went out in all weathers and often if the catch was good they had no time to eat. They did carry a tea can with a well fitting lid and a handle. The can was placed on the shrimp boiler and the coal shovel was used to fry bacon but they also nibbled away at hot shrimps.'

Barbara also dispelled one half-truth and that was that fishing in the Bay was rigidly seasonal. Shrimps and flatfish were caught in the spring, flatfish, salmon, sea bass and mullet in the summer, with shrimps and flatfish in the autumn. In the winter, flatfish which were always present in numbers were caught along with whiting, cod and whitebait.

'If the truth be told,' said Barbara, 'there was an overlap

Shrimp pickers (peelers), Morecambe, 1926.

and the techniques of fishing differed according to the product you were after. The problem was always one of marketing because there were slick operators who cheated the fishermen but thankfully there were not many of them. It was decided that a fishermen's cooperative would work together. This worked very well even though there was great rivalry among the families who always jostled with their nobbies to get to the best catches. What the cooperative did, however, was to negotiate the best price and the women, including those in my family, did their picking and processing under one roof. Every family's catch was carefully weighed and if you had a big catch there were eager pickers on hand to process the shrimps in time to catch the train. Everybody knew the going rate when the shrimps were sold and, even more importantly, the middlemen knew what they had to pay and could not bargain with individuals to keep the price down.'

The shrimping co-operative premises at Clarence Street.

Even though the fisherfolk worked hard to earn a living, there were times when catches were low and food had to be kept on the table. Once the holiday season was in full swing the nobbies were scrubbed, painted and extra seats provided for passengers eager to have a sail out into the Bay. The wealthy members of the Royal Windermere Yacht Club also employed the fishermen to crew their pleasure craft. The Morecambe lads all wanted to crew for Sir William Forewood, who was the Chairman of the Cunard company. Another source of income which soon developed was bed and breakfast. The cottage was spring-cleaned and the family moved out and lived in the sheds which were normally used to dry the nets.

Barbara Woodhouse mentioned that there was great rivalry between fishing families and I expected rivalry to be even fiercer between the villages. I thought, for example, there might have been pitched battles between the Morecambe families and those from Flookburgh. I put this to Barbara.

'No, this was not the case because the way we caught shrimps was different. We went out in our nobbies but most of the Flookburgh men went out on an ebbing tide and dragged a net through the water using firstly a horse and then a tractor. The prawns were also boiled in fresh and not sea water and so tasted different.'

This made sense because my wife and I went shrimping out of Flookburgh with our friend Harold Benson. My wife drove the tractor whilst Harold operated the net. At times he attached a trailer to the tractor and visitors could enjoy watching a shrimper at work. My job was to identify the other wildlife seen in the area and also to ensure that everyone, especially the children, was safe. At the end of the day Harold's family showed us how to 'peel' shrimps and what we did not need to be told was how to eat them!

I mentioned to Harold the rivalry between Morecambe fisher folk and those from Flookburgh.

'We were different,' he said, 'the only time we competed was in the marketing. We had our own cooperative, Flookburgh Fisheries Limited, which was founded by the Manning family and it worked very well. We did have fishing boats but these were not shrimpers and so we were different from the Morecambe lads although we did keep our distance. The only time you will ever get fishermen to work together is when our old enemy the sea gets a grip of any of us.'

Many Flookburgh folk are of Norse origin and even the name of the village sandwiched between the sea and the pretty little River Eea is Old Norse, once called Flokkisburgh. Here shrimping still goes on and many fishermen's cottages survive with the old stables attached and places where the shrimps were, and still are in a few cases, boiled.

Whilst museums do not completely tell the story of what the lives of local people were really like, some do a very good job. Among the best is the Lancaster Maritime Museum and I had a great deal of help for this book from Michelle Cooper, the assistant keeper, and, of course, from Barbara Woodhouse. As a guide she is perfect because she knows from experience what life was like. There is a display of inshore fishing such as musseling, cockling and shrimping. The lives of fishing families were centred upon the boat and the cottage kitchen, and there is a reconstruction of a typical kitchen dating to 1925 but which had changed little up to the 1970s. Look out also for the huge shrimp boiler which has already been mentioned as part of the nobby boats' furnishings. Most nobbies had a crew of two but Dick Woodhouse more often than not fished on his own. Like most of the 'Nobby Men', Dick Woodhouse was reluctant to give up sail for diesel and until his death in 1979 regarded himself as a skilled sailor – and so he was!

Until very recently fishermen saw themselves as a cross between conservationists and farmers. They knew that, in the long run, family fortunes were dependent upon conserving the breeding stocks. Each nobby carried sieves which allowed the young shrimps to pass through the mesh so that they could eventually spawn. Barbara Woodhouse once again had her finger firmly on the fishing pulse: 'We could see a problem coming from the 1960s onwards when bigger vessels began not just to trawl but actually to scrape the sea bottom in search of short term profits.'

Chapter 2

Lancashire's Coastal Fisheries

The whole of Lancashire's coastline from the Mersey to the Lune and Morecambe Bay consists of small sheltered bays. Here fishermen have, for centuries, combined the art of fishing (or should it be classed as a science?) with farming and handloom weaving. They were thus self-sufficient, with every member of the family helping to keep body and soul together. Each community kept itself to itself not because it wanted it so but largely because of geographical constraints in the days when the only mode of transport was by foot or by horse – and the creature was usually kept busy pulling the plough or cartloads of fish. In the days before refrigeration the surplus had to be sold or bartered as quickly as possible.

As we have seen, some families specialised in shrimping in purpose-built boats called nobbies which had a maximum crew of only two. Others operated larger boats, also built locally and to order, and these had more crew and made longer journeys in search of fish. One of these latter was the Leadbetter family and I was lucky enough to meet Ethel Chantler (née Leadbetter), who still works at the Fleetwood Museum.

'I've been associated with fishing all my life,' she told me. 'I was taught by my mother to be a net braider and I later married a man who became a successful trawler skipper out of Fleetwood. My ancestors were called Leadbetter and the family were owners of sailing smacks from the very beginning and had boats built in shipyards at Preston, Glasson Dock, Freckleton, Arnside, and a place which later became known as Fleetwood.'

Richard Leadbetter hailed originally from Marshside, near Southport, and was not just a successful fisherman but also very astute at business, a member of the council and a teetotal Methodist. He became known as 'Fish Dick' and owned Fleetwood post office, a large fish and chip shop in North Albert Street and the Bell Restaurant, as well as lots of houses. Fish Dick was no fishy character but a hardworking and religious man who even held services in his vessels. By the time he died in 1916 he had established a firm family business.

In 1893 he commissioned the Singleton Boat Yard in Fleetwood (in which he had shares) to build a vessel known as the *Harriet*, which some think was named after Fish Dick's daughter. The vessel cost £1,200 to build and the four-man crew, usually with a Leadbetter or two among them, could earn £2 per week which was a substantial wage in those days.

Ethel Chantler recalled:

'The *Harriet* must have been a wonderful boat because she made her last voyage in 1977 and was taken to the coast near Millom, in Cumbria, and converted into a day centre for handicapped children to be run by the Harriet Trust. This proved to be short lived as *Harriet* was showing her

Fisherman Henry Leadbetter of Fleetwood.

The Harriet *being built at Singleton's in the 1890s.*

age. She was a hulk by 1998 when the Friends and Staff of Fleetwood Museum succeeded in bringing her home. I had more than one tear in my eye as I saw a slice of my family history passing the Lower Lighthouse.'

Harriet has now been brought into the courtyard of the Fleetwood Museum and placed in a purpose-built hut which is also crammed full of fishing memorabilia and photographs. Dick Gillingham, another of the knowledgeable and hardworking staff of the museum, takes up the story:

'It is a real joy to be helping to preserve the *Harriet* which has now been registered by Greenwich and is a proud member of the National Register of Historic Vessels. She is the last surviving registered fishing smack operating from Fleetwood. She is a unique example of a type of vessel

The Margaret – *a Leadbetter vessel.*

which evolved specifically for work in the difficult waters of the Irish Sea and north-west coast. Fishing smacks were sail-driven but were without doubt the forerunners of the once massive trawler fleets. Technically she is a ketch-rigged fishing smack constructed of pitch pine planking on oak frames, 64 ft long with a beam of 21 ft and from keel to deck level, a height of 11 ft 9 inches. Her main mast was 45 ft high and her mizzen mast 27 ft high and she had a gross weight of 80 tons.'

Dick Gillingham likes nothing better than taking visitors on guided tours of the museum, including a stroll around the *Harriet*. I frequently went around during the researching of this book and was fascinated to be able to delve into the bowels of the vessel and get some insight into how the crew lived and worked during the long working life of the *Harriet*.
Dick went on:

'She usually had a crew of four plus a boy and she towed a beam trawl, which was a trawl net held open by a wooden beam weighted with iron "shoes" on either side.

The Harriet *crew in the 1940s.*

28

She had a full set of sails. She was initially totally dependent upon the wind and currents and had no power save that from a small steam boiler. This was used mainly to operate a capstan which helped to heave the trawl, which was hopefully heavy with fish. In the 1930s she was fitted with what was called a semi-diesel auxiliary which gave her a top speed of six knots. This helped the *Harriet* to negotiate the twists and turns of the inner harbour but her main propulsion was still sail and this was the case until after World War Two! In 1893 there were 60 deep sea smacks and 35 prawners working out of Fleetwood and as *Harriet* is the last of the latter we are all proud to be helping to preserve her.'

The Leadbetters were joined by other able and ambitious fishing families, including the Bettes clan who hailed from Padstow in Cornwall. They realised that the fish-rich waters of the Irish Sea and beyond would be more easily reached from the new and expanding port of Fleetwood and moved their operations lock, stock and barrel to the north-west. Here there was soon intermarriage between the Cornish and the locals and it soon became that if you kicked one they all limped. Many Cornish people made this journey and this included my own ancestors because Freethy is a Cornish name. One distant relative of mine was a fisherman in the 1890s but most were miners who found work in the coal mines of Lancashire as the tin mines of Cornwall declined. I still have a picture of Newlyn harbour given to me by my father when I was about ten, doing my share of cockling and shore fishing to supplement the family diet.

I will return to the history of sea fishing from trawlers later in the chapter but Lancashire has a long and distinguished history of harvesting the tides and coastal waters for fish. One of the most skilful of the surviving methods can be seen in the haaf netting of salmon. I once made a television film during which I had to be taught the skills of haaf netting and at the end of a tide I was exhausted whilst my teacher was as fit as a fiddle, apart from the muscles which he used to laugh! He was in his late seventies and I were nobbut a young 'un.

A typical haaf netter is a secretive soul until you get to know him and you can't blame him because salmon are valuable fish and getting to know the best places to fish takes years of experience, lots of patience and the ability to stand waist deep in cold water for hours. There are both spring and autumn runs of salmon in the Lune estuary close to Glasson Dock where I had my lesson before being warmed by a cup of tea laced with rum. I then talked to 90-year-old Deborah Benson whose father and grandfather had been haaf netters in Morecambe Bay. She told me:

'I don't know how long my family have fished hereabouts. My grandma told me proudly that there were Viking blood in my veins and all my brothers were haaf netters. The word haaf is a Norse word meaning 'sea' so the phrase just means 'a sea net'. You now know, Ron, how hard this is because you have been out and tried it. You caught one tiddler of a salmon and you did reet well to get one at all.

Haaf netters in unison.

Thomas Parkinson, lighthouse keeper, using his haaf net in 1946.

We've weighed yours at four pounds but some of my family have caught fish of up to 30 pounds.'

The net is basically purse-shaped, draped over a stout rod made of greenheart wood. Each is about 18 ft long, looking like a football goalpost and supported on three long pegs which fit over the shoulders. On an ebbing tide the net is carried like a yoke and the fisherman has to stand there but taking care not to sink into the mud. You cannot see the fish because the water is so cloudy but this also means that the salmon cannot see the net either. A skilled netter can feel when a salmon is caught and the net is lifted and the fish 'bagged'.

All haaf netters were, and still are, skilled fishermen with a deep knowledge of the sea, the tides and the shifting sands but, looked at in an historical sense, few were better than Thomas Parkinson, who was also the lighthouse keeper at Plover Scar off the coast of Cockerham in the 1940s. This lighthouse has sadly gone. It was built in 1847 and was an invaluable guide to vessels sailing in the shallow waters of the Lune estuary. Thomas was lucky in the sense that he earned part of his living from looking after the lighthouse and so he still had an income at times when the salmon were not running.

Betty Ousby remembered Thomas Parkinson:

'He were a grand netter but he were lucky that he had another job, but folk like my dad and brothers had to earn a crust when the salmon weren't running. We were whamellers, which were our name for drift netting. Most families had a 20-ft long drifter usually built at Arnside and we were either shrimpers or whamellers in search of fish. We had nets which were 300 yards long and 9 ft deep. They were weighted at the bottom with lead and kept afloat at the top with corks. They had to be kept in good condition and looked like huge net curtains when they were hung out to dry. They had to be spread all over with sticky waterproof stuff which smelled like tar and it was a mucky business. We also had smoke houses but these have nearly all gone. We used to have our own smoke house. This helped to preserve fish and mek it last longer so that selling were easier.'

Good haaf netters and whamellers knew where they could sell their produce and local hotels still have shrimps, fresh and smoked salmon and flatfish on their menu, including the Globe at Overton and the Golden Ball, on the road between Lancaster and Overton. The Golden Ball is also the place to watch the haaf netters at work and their nets and frameworks can be seen drying outside. In the old days the Golden Ball was known as 'Snatchems' because the Royal Navy's press gangs would occasionally raid the area and persuade local men – usually using a heavy stick – to join the men o' war.

Salmon is now a much sought after luxury and so is whitebait but this has not always been the case. In the early days of Lancashire's coastal fisheries, whitebait was a cheap food. One of the places I visit more than most is a port called Sunderland Point which is reached via a tidal causeway from Overton and is on the Lune estuary. Looking at my researches in 1970 I found the following account: 'I stood near the Butlers Packing Shed and spoke to the local fishermen and especially their children who were speaking as if they were in fairy land. An ancient and white-whiskered Peter Pan told me that the kids were picking strands of moonlight.' What these strands were was whitebait which is still found in numbers all around the Lancashire coast. The Packing Shed has long gone but whitebait is still on the menu, although is not now a staple item but an expensive starter.

At one time the Mersey between Liverpool and Warrington was an important area for fishing. In 1795 J. Aitken published *A Description of the Country for Thirty or Forty Miles around Manchester* and in this he mentioned that:

'The Mersey naturally is well stocked with fish and once afforded cheap food but the fish have diminished because of pollutants. This is true of the smelts and sparlings (whitebait) which annually in spring come up the river in huge shoals. There they spawn.'

The increase in pollution during the 18th, 19th and early 20th centuries virtually killed the fish in the river. In 1985 the then Conservative Government established the Mersey Basin Campaign with the object of restoring fish to the river. I was involved as the Scientific Director for some years and when the campaign was closed in 2010 there were fish, including salmon and whitebait, back in the river. My hope is that inshore fishing will once again become a means of producing locally-sourced food.

At one time there was a substantial fishing fleet based upon the Mersey estuary at Widnes and close to the Sankey Canal. It was

A young fisherman mending his nets at Glasson Dock.

all but destroyed by industrial pollution, especially the presence of a huge chemical complex, a reminder of which can be found in the Catalyst Museum which has been built on the site. This area has now been developed as an attractive country park. How strange it is that here at one time was the largest whitebait fishery in Europe, to be followed later by the largest chemical complex in Europe. There are still fishing boats in the area and who knows, this activity may eventually thrive and thus complete the circle in the history of the Lancashire fishing industry.

Now it's time to return to the history of deep-sea fishing, as opposed to coastal fishing in Lancashire, and once again I was able to speak to Ethel Chantler.

'Most of the established fishing families like mine expected that steam would eventually take over from sail but it took until 1891 before anyone dare risk buying purpose-built vessels. It made financial sense to delay as long as possible because there were a lot of sailing vessels like the *Harriet* which were already operating at a good profit. If I remember rightly the first steam vessel to come into Fleetwood was the *Lark* and she came from Grimsby to try her luck. The *Lark* was 99 ft long, weighed 133 tons and was built in Sunderland. Her skipper was Harry Bird and he moved to Fleetwood with all his family and they soon settled down among us because all fisher folk have a common shared bond of facing the danger of the sea.'

Trawler owners from Grimsby and especially Hull knew that Lancashire coal was cheaper and Moody and Kelly's Grimsby Steam Fishing Company developed what became known as a fleet of 'IC' trawlers. These were the *Arctic*, *Baltic*, *Celtic*, *Electric*, *Frolic* and *Gaelic*, plus even more 'ics'!

The Kelsall and Beeching fleet moved from Hull and established their 'Birdy' vessels, including *Grouse*, *Jay*, *Swift* and *Wren*. By 1897 the Fleetwood fleet of steam trawlers had increased to 32 and by this time the Marr family had also moved from Hull; James J. Marr brought five trawlers to Fleetwood and never looked back. The Marr vessels were called *Marrs*, *Lucerne*, *Annie*, *Akranes* and *Rattler*. Soon the *Amy* and the *Maud* were added and the Marrs have been part of the Lancashire steam trawling industry perhaps more than any other family.

Joseph Marr was a man of ambition and a marketing genius. He realised that hake was actually an edible fish and not one to be discarded and either dumped at sea or sold as offal. He marketed the species so well that it put Fleetwood firmly on the fishing map. I do honestly believe that Joseph Marr saved the Fleetwood industry almost single-handedly. In 1897 Kelsall and Beechings had removed all of their 32 vessels back to Hull and the prospects for the Lancashire port were bleak indeed. Two factors saved the port – Joseph and the hake.

Piscatorial historians echo this opinion. A skipper called Pearson Colley (a good name for a fisherman?) originally sent two boxes of hake to Manchester and a man by the equally evocative name of Theophilus Handley bought the lot and wanted more. Then Joseph Marr took over and his publicity was first-class, as he marketed hake as a luxury item which fish and chip shops and restaurants embraced with alacrity. There was soon an insatiable demand for hake from Fleetwood and there is no doubt that this was the main factor accounting for this west coast port becoming the third most important fish market in Britain behind Grimsby

A sturgeon caught on the Lune off Glasson Dock, displayed outside Nicholsons Boatyard.

and Hull. By 1910 there were more than 100 steam trawlers operating out of Fleetwood and, whilst the Marrs led the way, other companies were also successfully operating and providing jobs for newcomers and folk coming to the town in search of well paid, if physically hard, jobs.

At the same time, families like the Leadbetters and their sailing smack the *Harriet* were still operating and catching other species of fish to be sold at the early morning auctions which had road and rail links to the large towns and cities. Fleetwood was now a fishing port to rival all the others, but also had an extra dimension in that it was close to Blackpool and could enjoy a spin off from the town of fun and frolic and double as a tourist resort.

Chapter 3

The Growth of Fleetwood

In the very early days the Hesketh family from their base at Rossall Hall (now a public school) had done their best to be self-sufficient. In the late 1700s, with their farms proving to be very efficient, they funded the construction of a small fleet of

The Fleetwood fishing fleet, circa 1890.

inshore fishing vessels based on the sloping sands of Rossall beach. A succession of severe storms in 1814 persuaded Bold Hesketh, the then Lord of the Manor, to move the fleet into the shelter of the Wyre estuary long before Peter Hesketh-Fleetwood, who was his nephew, built the town of Fleetwood.

Bold built huts for his fishermen to live in and this was the seed from which modern Fleetwood has grown. At that time there were two small ports higher up the river with Wardley Creek on one bank and Skipool on the other. The Romans had also had a port, called *Portus Setantiorum*, which has long vanished beneath the sea but was almost certainly in the area between Fleetwood and Knott End.

I spoke at length and over numerous cups of tea with Dick Gillingham, who lectures frequently on the history of the area. He told me:

'By 1840 an extensive channel had been surveyed by a Captain Denham and an ingenious system of four lighthouses was constructed to guide vessels into Fleetwood Docks. Two of these lights survive. The lights were switched on together on 20th June 1840 and wild celebrations were held. Pilots were in position off the Lune Deeps and to allow these efficient men to remain active whilst they were waiting for cargoes they were allowed to fish and to sell their catch on the docks. They established the Fleetwood Fishing Company and this proved to be even more lucrative than piloting. They were soon able to finance their own purpose-built vessels and the pilot cutters were very profitable.'

The port itself was the dream of one man, Peter Hesketh-Fleetwood, aided by one of the greatest architects in Britain. In the 1830s Fleetwood was watching the railway push its way towards the Lancashire coast and after carefully studying the latest engineering techniques, he formed the opinion that it would be impossible to drive a line up, over and down Shap Fell into

Scotland. He therefore employed the architect Decimus Burton –
one of John Nash's most able pupils – to design a new town to be
built at the mouth of the Wyre and to provide a rail link and a
steamer route into Scotland. Why the name Decimus? This was
because his parents were prolific and Decimus was his father's
tenth son! Why Burton? Fleetwood Hesketh knew that he was the
best, having designed London's Regent Street, as well as large
areas of St Leonard's-on-Sea and Hove.

Dick Gillingham went on:

'In the context of the Lancashire fishing industry, the only
thing which is relevant is the dockland area and, of course,
the two splendid lighthouses which still stand proudly
overlooking the sea. The railway did reach Fleetwood and
at its terminus Burton built the North Euston Hotel and
Fleetwood Hesketh awaited a flood of passengers taking
passage to Scotland. All looked to be progressing from the
opening day in 1847 and it was visited by Queen Victoria
on her way to Scotland. Poor old Fleetwood Hesketh got
only one thing wrong. This was also the year in which
railway engineers succeeded in building a line over Shap
Fell and on to Scotland and his dream became a nightmare.
Two factors saved the new town from crumbling away to
dust. One was the development of the town into a seaside
resort, but even more important was the expansion of the
deep sea fishing industry.'

It was actually the expanding railway network which was
literally Fleetwood's lifeline. The demand for cheap fish by the
mill towns whose populations were increasing at great speed
meant that demand often exceeded supply. In those days price
rises were not the only answer to shortages and to increase
supply new and larger vessels – trawlers in the true sense of
the word – were being added to the fleet. More fish meant
more profits.

The 1851 census shows that Fleetwood's population was

already over 3,000 and was expanding quickly, with the livelihood of many people being totally dependent upon fishing. Fish auctions were held on an almost daily basis with the exception of Sundays. Fish wagons were specifically designed and attached to trains and despatched to the hungry towns. Mary Bowes remembers:

'As a child in the 1930s we lived close to the railway near to Preston and the trains puffed along slowly at the points from where they could then be directed to the various towns. My father worked on the railway and so I knew what was going on. I can still remember the smell which wafted in through my bedroom window early in the morning as the fish wagons were being sent on their way to the chip shops all over the county and into Yorkshire.'

From 1860 these fish wagons had been busy and growth was continual. From 32 vessels operating at this time the number had doubled by 1876 and the combined weight of fish and shellfish leaving the docks exceeded 100 tons per day.

It was apparent that the nobbies were too small and the larger fishing smacks such as the *Harriet* already described were venturing into deeper waters. These new vessels landed skate, hake, cod and dogfish, which was also known as rock salmon. All fishermen were delighted when they caught edible crabs because these commanded a very high price.

The temptation today, as we look at the huge foreign trawlers, is to think that the old smacks were not much more than rowing boats with sails. This is far from the truth as Derek Keetley, who became a trawler skipper out of Grimsby, told me:

'The smacks towed a 50-ft wide beam trawl net attached to 150 fathoms (900 ft) of rope. This generated work for net and rope makers. The smacks were sail powered and this generated work for linen workers and sail makers. This is why fishing ports provided work for fishermen's wives and families and attracted lots of incomers in search of employment.'

The trawler by its very definition has to drag a huge net through the water and in the days of sail needed a strong wind to propel it. These vessels needed a very skilful skipper to judge the wind. The trawl net also required great skills in its construction and was held open by a heavy wooden beam with even heavier weights. It needed very fit and agile young men to heave a net full of fish even though they later had powered winches to help.

Dick Gillingham told me of a very significant change in the design of the equipment:

'The real change began around 1894 when the beam trawls were replaced by otter boards. These proved more efficient and therefore cost effective but some skippers took a long time to be convinced. Superficially the two trawls look similar but the heavy wooden beam was a real problem because it was too solid and also restricted the width of the net. This was replaced by a pair of separated structures called otter boards which could move apart and gradually open the net as the weight of the catch increased. Once reluctant skippers realised that they could catch more fish in each trawl they accepted the change, which improved their income. This invention coincided with the advent of the steam-powered trawlers which were obviously not dependent upon the wind and could move faster and manoeuvre more easily. These vessels could venture into deeper colder waters where there were huge shoals of fish. The first vessel to use these combined fishing methods was a trawler called the *Otter* and this accounts for the name of otter boards. They were also known as trawl doors.'

As already mentioned, Fleetwood's first steam trawler, called the *Lark*, arrived in 1891, three years before the otter boards came into operation. The *Lark* was owned by Moody and Kelly, a Grimsby company, and Derek Keetley, a proud Grimsby lad himself, recalled,

'The *Lark* must have been a sturdy craft because she was built in the 1880s and sailed for several years out of Fleetwood. Eventually she was sold to a Burmese company and was scrapped in 1936.'

This change in trawler design can be seen by comparing the make-up of Fleetwood's fishing fleet between 1893 and 1912. During my long conversations with Ethel Chantler over gallons of tea she made a very valid point:

'I know your book is called *Memories of the Lancashire Fishing Industry* but you'll be surprised to find out how long the memories of fishing families actually are, and I can remember discussions round our table talking about changes long before the First World War. I remember conversations with my father and grandfather about the changes in the boats as sail was replaced by steam. I was told that in 1893 there were nearly 100 sailing trawlers operating out of Fleetwood and there were 34 left at the start of the first war. They also mentioned the changes which took place in the design of the fish docks and quays.'

Following Ethel's advice I looked up the details of the new docks. The Wyre dock was opened in 1877 and provided deeper berthing facilities and thus attracted larger vessels, some dealing with commerce rather than fishing. The fishing fleet was reluctant to move because at their smaller Jubilee Dock they did not have to pay any berthing fees.

Gradually, however, things changed as fishing vessels increased in size and they could unload their catch more quickly and so return to the sea within a day or so. A trawler not catching fish was what we would describe in modern terms as a declining asset!

As we have seen, in 1893 the Hull-based company Kelsall Brothers and Beeching operated a fleet of 32 steam trawlers but only four years later they abandoned Fleetwood and returned to Hull. Fleetwood, however, rode this storm as Dick Gillingham told me:

'1898 was a watershed year for Fleetwood as the Marr family started operating from the town. William Marr was born in Dundee and was a harpooner aboard a whaling vessel. He died at sea and was buried in Greenland, leaving behind a son whom he had never seen. Joseph Marr began life as a simple fish curer but in 1870 he built his own fishing smack called the *Adelaide*. By 1887 he had eight trawlers operating out of Hull which then had 448 vessels berthed in the port. At that time most owners were convinced – economically at least – that steam trawlers would never replace sail. They were wrong! Steam trawlers certainly cost more to run as they had to pay for fuel and had larger crews but as we have seen briefly already they had one very great advantage. They were not at the mercy of the wind for motive power and could fish in all but the very worst of weather conditions. They could also tow much larger nets because they had so much extra power. The Marr family had the commonsense to appreciate the value of steam and James Herbert Marr joined his father and they built the steam

James Herbert Marr, 1912.

Lionel Marr in the galley of the Jacinta.

trawler *Marrs* which was 100-ft long and had a gross weight of 100 tons. By 1898 they had decided to base their operations at Fleetwood and to use the Wyre dock for their vessels. Profits soared and there are still Marrs in Fleetwood today.'

There is no doubt that fishing family dynasties like the Marrs and others were the life blood of all the major fishing ports of Britain.

The Fleetwood fishing fleet continued to expand until 1914, when the First World War disrupted the industry as many trawlers were converted into minesweepers and the U-boat threat restricted the movement of those old and slow-moving trawlers which remained. This was also the case in the Second World War but the reduction in fishing over a period of more than four years resulted in a rapid recovery of fish stocks. With the peace in 1918 came a demand for a varied diet and fish was high on the menu. All looked bright for the fishing ports and the only problems

Fleetwood had become a major port by 1900.

resulted from the need to replace sunk, damaged and ancient trawlers. However, add to this the inevitable arguments between ambitious men in search of profits and you have something of a storm in potentially calm waters. One such storm occurred in Lincolnshire which turned out to be of some benefit to Fleetwood. Between the wars a trawler fleet was established in Liverpool but this did not survive for very long.

The Boston Fish Party

On the face of it, it would seem that events taking place far away at Boston in Lincolnshire in 1926 would not impact in any way on the Fleetwood fishing fleet but this proved not to be the case and many folk still have memories of the knock-on effect of a very heated legal battle.

In 1922 Fred Parkes had become chairman of the Boston Deep Fishing and Ice Company which had dominated the fishing in a town establishing itself as a major fishing port to rival the East Coast fleets at Grimsby and Hull. That year, a colliery vessel called *The Lockwood* lost her steering gear and grounded in the River Witham, thus blocking the entrance to Boston Harbour. The harbourmaster approached the Boston Deep Fishing and Ice Company, asking for help. The trawler *William Brown* succeeded in refloating the collier but as the tide ebbed she grounded once more. Matters were made worse when she capsized and it was when she had to be salvaged that the wrangling began. A Grimsby company was approached but their quote was too high and the harbour commissioners employed Fred Parkes. When Fred sent in his bill the Harbour Commissioners refused to pay and the only winners, as has always been usual in these cases, were likely to be the lawyers.

Fred Parkes reacted by moving his operations lock, stock and barrel to Fleetwood, but he decided to retain the name of the company. It seems strange to relate that at one time the Boston Deep Fishing and Ice Company had no fewer than 82 steam trawlers operating out of Fleetwood and they also had vessels at Hull, Grimsby, Aberdeen and Lowestoft. Never again did the company operate out of Boston. How this town, now in a backwater, would have prospered had it not been for the 'Boston Fish Party' we will never know. The Boston enterprise involved deep water trawling over very long distances and into often perilous seas.

This was certainly a boost for Fleetwood but by then the port had already become important as a distant-water trawler port. Serious deep-water trawling began slowly in 1889 when a vessel appropriately called the *Stormcock* brought a load of mackerel and herring into the Wyre dock, which at that time was mainly concerned with other imports, especially grain and timber. Steam trawlers were also becoming more important and the timber pond and the grain elevator had to be sacrificed as more and more fish were being landed.

In the 1890s a group of Grimsby trawler owners established a deep water fishery which obtained most of its catch from the waters around Iceland and were in need of a West Coast berthing facility. Derek Keetley told me:

'Fleetwood was ideal because it was closer to the rich fishing grounds and had a good railway network which Fleetwood Hesketh had developed. I have a number of friends who describe themselves as "Piscatorial

Historians" who are still enthralled by the rise and fall of the fishing industry.'

The big trawlers were no threat to the local fishermen because there were three distinct fleets operating out of Fleetwood. There was the inshore fleet, which as we have seen were mostly family-owned and landed mainly prawns, flat fish and estuary salmon. Then there developed the middle-water trawlers which worked out of local waters but were prepared to venture out into Scottish waters and perhaps as far as the Faroes, and catches here included hake, whiting, cod and even ray, which like the dogfish was a member of the shark family. The distant-water trawlers had crews of up to 20 real tough guys who could remain at sea in Arctic conditions for up to a month at a time depending upon the amount of fish caught. They fished around Iceland, the White Sea, Bear Island and off the coast of Norway, often in the depths of winter. Catches included cod, plaice, sole, haddock, and my own favourite which is halibut, which cuts like steak but tastes like fish.

Fishermen working in these conditions need all the friends they can get and since 1865 one of the best of the *Fisherman's Friends* has been their favourite strong-tasting lozenge, which is still made in the town and thanks to skilful advertising is world famous. In 1865 James Lofthouse, a Fleetwood pharmacist, was so popular with fishermen seeking relief from bronchial complaints with his liquid produced from a secret recipe that his own shop became too small. The business is still owned by the family and is now housed in a modern and huge factory on the outskirts of the town. Initially, the liquid was a problem since it had to be sold in glass bottles which were often broken during rough seas. James Lofthouse solved this by soaking a rich dough in the liquid and pressing this mixture into tablets which were then baked. The precise recipe is still a closely-guarded secret but in the mixture are liquorice, capsicum, eucalyptus and menthol.

The Lofthouse family is a vital part of the history of Fleetwood but so are the families of the trawler owners and the men who crewed the ships.

Chapter 4

The Trawlers

In the early days each fisherman had his own family boat which he maintained himself. Gradually, the more able men could afford additional boats and to employ crews to fish for them. These crews were wage earners and therefore had no share in the profits.

Just before the Depression came in the 1930s there were 200 fishing vessels operating out of Fleetwood and this was reduced to 112 as hard times took their toll. At that time the number of owners fell from 60 to 21. It really was a case of the survival of the fittest. Both skill and bravery were needed to literally stay afloat. One family which rode the storm was the Marrs, who have already been mentioned. Despite the Depression there were a few other far-sighted owners who actually moved into Fleetwood at this difficult time. These companies, including the Hewitt Fishing Company, saw the economic benefit of operating out of Fleetwood because it was closer to the lucrative fishing grounds and therefore reduced fuel costs. The Hewitts were the oldest established fishing company in England and at one time they had more than 200 sailing smacks working out of several east coast ports. The company cleverly kept abreast of new developments in trawler design and so had competitive fleets. They also had links with London's Billingsgate fish market.

The same could be said for the MacFisheries fleet of 'Northern' trawlers – the names of the fleet always began with *Northern*. This fleet joined forces with the Hewitt vessels and many were built in German shipyards which, from a crewman's point of view, meant they were more spacious and comfortable than the British-designed trawlers. This was noted by the Admiralty who at the start of 1939 requisitioned these boats as minesweepers, which often confused the German U-boat captains who thought that they were friendly vessels, especially when seen in poor weather and with a heavy sea running.

Another company which moved into Fleetwood in the early 1930s was the Iago Steam Trawler Company Limited. This was founded by Commander E.D.W. Lawford, whose first trawler was named *Iago* and it was from this that the company took its name. I was lucky enough to spend some time eating cake and drinking tea with Mrs Joyce Openshaw, now in her nineties, who is the daughter of Commander Lawford and, for some time, was herself a director of the Iago Company. Few men can have served both in the Royal Navy and the Fishing Industry as did Edward Lawford. He was awarded the DSO for his bravery during the PQ 17 Convoy to Russia in 1942 and decorated with an OBE in 1962 for his services to the trawler industry.

Captain Lawford.

Joyce Openshaw told me:

'My father entered the Navy in 1911 and served in destroyers throughout World War One. He fought in the Battle of Jutland in 1916 and during this action a shell landed close to him and fractured his eardrum. Around 1920 he was invalided out of the Navy and

49

used his pension to purchase two trawlers which he sailed out of Milford Haven. These vessels were built by Hellyer Brothers of Hull and were 100-ft long steam trawlers. The first of these vessels was *Iago*, named after the Shakespearian character in *Othello*. The company was very successful and by the time the decision was made to relocate to Fleetwood there was a fleet of ten trawlers. My father's reason for moving his base was that he was sure that the Fleetwood running costs would be lower and there was also a deep reservoir of excellent fishermen all eager to work if they were properly treated.'

The Iago policy of looking after their crewmen was at the time revolutionary; there was some conscious effort to create a family feeling not only within each ship but in the fleet as a whole. I have spoken to many of the men who went to sea under the Iago flag and they all agreed that this was the case. Harry Chantler, who became a skipper in the 1950s at the very tender age of only 23, told me:

'I never wanted to work for anybody else. Iago spent time and money on the trawlers and their crews and did not squeeze every penny out of the business. Life at sea has always been tough and the more comforts you can have on board the easier it is to survive and work to the best of your ability.'

Lawford was a fierce advocate for doing away with the cramped accommodation on the trawlers and insisted on the provision of better living and working quarters, most of it being placed aft of the forecastle. He worked on this all through the 1930s and, by the start of the 1939 war, all of the Iago fleet of twelve trawlers were in prime condition and were quickly requisitioned by the Admiralty for use as escort vessels and especially as minesweepers.

Commander Lawford was himself 'requisitioned' and, given the rank of Captain, was quite willing to be thrust into a new and potentially deadly conflict. His knowledge of both destroyers and trawlers saw him ideally placed to be involved in the Anti-submarine Division. In 1941 he supervised the conversion of a banana boat which was renamed HMS *Pozarica* and went to war as an anti-aircraft vessel. In June 1942 she sailed in great haste and secrecy as part of the Convoy PQ17 to Russia. This sudden departure trapped on board a young journalist called Godfrey Winn, who subsequently wrote a book called *PQ17* and which chronicles Captain Lawford's gallant handling of his ship in these dangerous and freezingly cold waters. In 1942 Lawford was awarded the DSO for his 'outstanding services'.

In 1945, at the conclusion of hostilities, Lawford returned to Fleetwood to resume his trawler operations. The fact that he succeeded so well is a tribute to his own drive and ability but also to the quality and loyalty of his skippers and their crews.

The Iago Company first bought two modern trawlers, the *Red Knight* and the *Red Lancer*, and other vessels soon followed as the Fleetwood vessels took a leading role in the landing of fish of a wide variety of species as Britain recovered from the hungry days of the war. Just how dominant the Iago Company became can be seen by listing the total catch between 1947 and 1957:

Company	Number of boxes landed
The Iago Steam Trawling Company	1,549,751
Hewett Fishing Company	1,205,893
Wyre Trawlers Limited	1,203,858
James Marr and Sons Limited	893,620

There were also ten other smaller companies operating out of Fleetwood, at that time a booming port.

Along with the pressing need for better accommodation for the crews, the Iago policy was to build the new vessels to the highest standards and also to fit the latest technological improvements. Lawford built two new oil-fired trawlers, constructed in Aberdeen. One was the *Red Rose* and the other the *Red Hackle* and they both had built-in radar. These were the first two vessels fitted with radar to operate out of Fleetwood. Then came the diesel-powered trawlers *Captain Riou* which was completed in 1957, *Captain Hardy* in 1958, *Captain Freemantle* in 1959, and in 1960 *Captain Foley* and *Captain Inman* joined the Iago fleet. The names of these vessels were taken from the list of Lord Nelson's captains who fought with him at the Battle of Trafalgar in October 1805.

Each company had its own unique colour pattern on their superstructures, their flags and their funnels. Joyce Openshaw, who was at that time a director of the Iago Company, remembers this period vividly:

'In the 1940s I designed the house flag of the Iago Steam Trawler Company which was black with a prominent red band, which was also painted on the funnels of all our vessels. I still laugh at one of my father's memories which was a postal order from the Admiralty for the princely sum of 6d (2½ pence). This was part of the salvage money relating to the Battle of Jutland in 1916. Such is the lesson to be learned with reference to inflation and I still wonder what proportion of this large sum was used to set up the Iago fleet. In 1963 when my father retired I was already a director of the company but we could also see that hard times were coming. It made economic sense to sell out to the Boston Deep Sea Fisheries Company and I have never ever regretted this decision.'

In March 2010 I visited Fleetwood Docks in the company of Dick Gillingham, a man fascinated by the history of Fleetwood. He showed me a building at the edge of the Wyre dock overlooked by a modern marina complex and told me that this was the one remaining office block belonging to a trawling company. This was once the working base for the Iago Company and one which would have been fondly remembered by Joyce Openshaw.

There is no doubt that the Iago Company was one of only a few which embraced new design and technology. I remember in the

The one-time offices of the Iago trawling company.

early 1990s sitting on a seat overlooking the Fleetwood-Knott End ferry with my mother who was approaching 90 and had clearer memories of the past than she had of her latter years. As she watched a small fishing boat set out into the channel she suddenly started to talk about her father who she described as a ship's engineer. Engineer was not his original title because he began life on a sailing ship and later became a fireman stoker aboard merchant ships and steam trawlers. This must literally have been one hell of a job because shovelling coal into a boiler all day must have been as hot as Old Nick's Den itself!

My mother told me that grandad had a burn on his arm which was caused by carbide. I thought that this was strange until I read that when water is dropped onto carbide, acetylene gas is produced. It burns with a bright flame but if the burning is not controlled a lethal explosion is the result. Dick Gillingham told me:

'The steam trawler *Betty Johnson* had an accident with carbide which was used to provide light for the vessel and three men were killed. There are also side effects of breathing in acetylene, including violent headaches, and the stink is awful and makes your eyes water.'

The engine room men were always in the bowels of the ship and therefore had to deal with acetylene but at least they were warm and dry and they preferred to sleep in their workplace rather than turn into a freezing cold and damp bunk.

When coal boilers were replaced by more efficient fuels, things got easier for the engine room men. Gone were the dirt, the dust and the sheer physical effort of shovelling heavy coal into boilers as the sea rolled violently enough to have hot coals spilling out. Many trawler owners, however, were reluctant to abandon coal as a fuel because some had bought shares in the Lancashire coal mines and therefore had easy access to cheap supplies. This remained the case until after 1947 when the mines were nationalised.

Once liquid fuels, especially diesel, literally came on stream, engineers began to take a pride in polished brasses and clean floors, and apart from smudges of oil their personal appearance improved. They had an easier life but despite improvements to the conditions endured by the fish men the engineers kept

The Lord Lloyd, *the last coal-fired trawler, scrapped in 1963.*

Ships of the Iago Steam Trawler Co. Fleet, 1958-62.

themselves apart and nestled comfortably in their warm and cleaner quarters.

I have spoken at length to many trawler skippers who fished from the 1950s onwards including Derek Keetley of Grimsby and Harry Chantler of Fleetwood. Both said that the engine room chaps and the fishing crew were very different and there was an accepted demarcation between them. The fish men were always tired and tended to take the engineers for granted. After all, all they had to do was to keep the trawler moving at the right speed. They did not, and some still do not, realise what a skilled job it is to keep an engine running at its most economical in terms of fuel and also to be able to carry out repairs on the spot and quickly.

'Any skipper will tell you,' said Derek Keetley, 'that a stationary trawler costs everybody money. I know that at sea I was the god above, but there was an oily devil below that it made sense to keep happy.'

Trawler Design

The new designs of the trawlers from the 1960s onwards are described in the publicity material produced by John Lewis and Sons Ltd of Aberdeen. It is dated 24th May 1960 and is worth quoting in full:

'The Motor Trawler *Captain Foley* is the latest addition to the trawler fleet operated by Messrs Iago Steam Trawler Company Ltd from Fleetwood. She is the eighth motor trawler to be built for this company by Messrs John Lewis and Sons Limited, in recent years and is the tenth post-war trawler so to be built. *Captain Foley* is, therefore, the result of years of cooperation between the owners and the builders and it would be true to say that she is an outstanding trawler of her type. Built for the "middle water fishing grounds" from Fleetwood with the hake market particularly in view, she was launched from the builder's shipyard today.

Full steam ahead for the Anchorite *in the late 1950s; a James Marr and Sons vessel.*

'Like other recently-built ships for these owners, this ship bears the name of one of Lord Nelson's famous captains. From outward appearance the *Captain Foley* is in accordance with the present-day practice for motor trawlers and yet is unmistakably one of the Iago Fleet. The special features outwardly are the raked soft nosed stem, well-flared bow, raised bulwark in way of the working deck, large wheelhouse and searchlights above and deep cruiser stern. A lavender grey hull was also distinctive of the owning company. At night the decks are a blaze of light from the floodlights, searchlights and fluorescent deck lighting system.

'Internally the features which would attract most attention for those connected with the fishing industry would perhaps be the fish room, engine room and the crew's accommodation. The fish room is sheathed on the sides and bulkheads with aluminium alloy sheeting. The fish room posts are of galvanised steel and the division and shelf boards are of aluminium alloy. The floor is cement on cork insulation. The aim is to be able to carry fish in thoroughly hygienic conditions and to minimise the work necessary to maintain these conditions.

'The engine room is spacious with plenty of space for access and maintenance of the main and auxiliary machinery. The lighting is by means of fluorescent strip lighting and the ventilation by means of electrically driven forced draft fans situated in a separate fan room in the bridge structure. The platform and floor plates are of aluminium alloy.

'The main engine is a direct drive, direct reversing diesel engine by Messrs British Polar Company Ltd, Glasgow, their M.N.S. 6 cylinder turbo charged engine developing 1250 B.h.p. at 250 r.p.m. This power will mean that the *Captain Foley* will be one of the most powerful middle water trawlers afloat.

'Accommodation is provided amidships and aft for 19

men. The wheelhouse, chartroom and captain's cabin are on the bridge deck. The wheelhouse, which is partly constructed of aluminium alloy has strengthened windows, Kent clear view screen projector, compass, Marconi radio locator Radar, DECCA Navigator, Marconi Fishgraft and Scavisa II Echo Sounders, Talk Back, S.R.E and hand hydraulic steering pedestal. The chart room contains Marconi Transarctic radio telephone, S.S.L Trawling Log is fitted.

'The Captain's bathroom adjoins his cabin. These spaces are provided with steam heating and forced draft ventilation. Below the bridge accommodation are single berth cabins for mate and wireless operator and the officers' bathroom. Going aft from these cabins by means of an enclosed alleyway lit by fluorescent lighting, one reaches the engine room, galley and mess room. The galley contains an oil fired vitreous enamel finished stove with twin forced draft fans and stainless steel fittings. An electrically driven potato peeler is installed. The furniture is of teak and plastic material and the deck tiled. The mess room furniture is of polished oak with bulkheads of plastic. The engineers and the remainder of the crew have cabins on the upper deck, aft and the cabin flat. All these cabins are furnished in polished light oak, steam heated and ventilated by electrically driven fans which are situated in the steering gear compartment.

Technical Detail – *Captain Foley*

Registered Length	139' 5"
Length	136' 0"
Breadth	28' 0"
Tonnage	440 tons
Fish room Capacity	10,000 cubic ft'

It is interesting to have the comments of skippers and crew who welcomed these new designs with their increased comforts and safety devices. Harry Chantler, who sailed for Iago out of

Fleetwood, told me:

'When you read this spec. it is no wonder that there was always a queue of trawlermen waiting at the Iago desk when a new vessel was about to be added to the fleet. For the first time the deckhands could be dry and warm between their few off-duty hours. They would stay healthy and have a longer working life.'

Derek Keetley, who skippered the 'new' trawlers out of Grimsby, agreed:

'Having a crew feeling comfortable made the skipper's job easier and the new electronic equipment was exciting, and you also knew where the fish were by echo sounding. As equipment improved we also learned to identify various species. I only ever sailed in these new vessels but I've spoken to the old time skippers and deckhands and life was a lot tougher for them.'

Mick Rodgers spent all of his working life as a crewman on Fleetwood trawlers and knows more than most about how tough life was out at sea. He told me:

'When I think of my days as a galley boy those new galleys were a joy to work in. They were not only easier to clean but a lot safer and designed to cope with rough seas, with ledges and devices to hold things steady. I always look at my arthritic hands and think of spuds in cold water and then of an electric potato peeler. Life were much easier then but one thing never changes – that's the sheer bloody strength of the sea.'

Mick Rodgers never said a truer word. There was a real threat from the sea and the next chapter concerns itself with the memories of the brave men who worked on the trawler fleet.

Chapter 5

The Crewmen

To say that life was tough for all the trawlermen is something of an understatement. Accommodation aboard was cramped, the sea was often rough and always cold and this combination meant that working conditions were hazardous.

In the days of the steam trawlers there were tiers of bunks on either side with a mess table between. There was a small solid fuel stove which was barely adequate even in normal conditions, never mind in the depths of the ice-bound Arctic. The crew were seldom dry and colds must have been a problem. It is no wonder that Fisherman's Friends, already described, were in such great demand.

On deck the conditions were always hazardous and the men very often had to work waist deep in swirling water as waves swept over the gunwales. If a warp on the nets snapped, the twisting metal was hurled around and was quite capable of cutting a man in two. Trawlermen, however, had seawater in their blood, muscle and every bodily sinew and accepted these hazards as a necessary aspect of their lives.

One of the most dangerous phases was that involved in hauling in the net. The winch would be started as water was squeezed from every strand and blew about in an icy wind. The sounds of birds and rattling chains were often deafening and the otter doors were raised from the waters and the gallows shackled: the gallows was a metal framework on which the net was supported.

It was the duty of the mate to release the knots securing the net and allow the fish to cascade onto the deck and then into the well of the fish deck. All this work was often carried out in a heavy swell and it is no small wonder that so many fishermen had missing fingers or scars caused by crushing. Down below there was gutting to be done and the fish packed in ice boxes, called pounds.

In addition to the fishing, the vessel had to be kept safe and on most voyages icing was a regular hazard. If the ice gathered on the rigging, this weight affected the balance of the trawler, making it top heavy, and there was a real danger of capsizing. No deckhand needed persuading to take part in chopping off the ice despite the fact that it was a dangerous and a most uncomfortable operation. The crew had to work hard and at high speed to remove the potentially lethal load.

Working on the mid-water trawlers was physically very hard but at least the crew did not have to cope with arctic weather.

The crewing of a trawler, under the skipper, falls into three categories – fishers, engineers and cooks. The latter, I was told, could make or break a voyage and once I realised just how tough the life at sea was I could see how important good, hot food became. A young boy entered the fishing team as a deckie learner and once his early apprenticeship was over he became a deckhand. The good men rose to become third hands, who were known as bosuns. The next promotion was to mate and finally to skipper. Some skippers began their sea life as galley boys, who could later become either chief cook or go out on deck and begin to climb the promotion ladder. The chief engineer learned a different set of skills altogether and few, if any, ever became, or indeed wanted to become, skippers. One loved engines and the other catching fish and the livelihood of each depended upon the efficiency of the other. In the early coal-fuelled trawlers, engineers began as 'trimmers', whose job was to keep the coal supply on line for those who stoked the boilers.

Enormous amounts of fuel were needed on the long voyages and space for coal was at a premium. The problem was solved by storing coal for the outward journey in the fish room which was then scrubbed clean before being filled with fish. The bunkered coal was used for the return journey. As diesel engines were introduced the greasers replaced the firemen, with the more efficient and ambitious moving up to become second and then chief engineers.

Life on board a trawler was cramped and on long voyages men's tempers were apt on occasions to become short. There was sometimes banter between the deckhands who had to stand long, cold watches and also to work in tough freezing conditions whilst fishing, and the engineers who had no watches except over their engines which kept them warm. On the whole, however, a trawler was a happy, hard-working vessel.

A deckhand was not, as the uninitiated may imagine, an unskilled toughie, but had to be quick thinking and competent in several skills, including compass reading and steering, repairing nets, tying knots, splicing rope and wire, identifying species and sorting the catch into sizes, gutting and cleaning the fish and removing the livers which were kept separately to make oil. The trawlers had special drums for the liver oil which was an extra source of income to be shared between owners and crew.

Some deckhands became specialists in particular skills and I was told that a good fish room man was worth his weight in gold and he had two men working under him. Prior to starting fishing, slats of wood were inserted across the decking to produce square boxes called pounds and these stopped the fish from sliding about and bruising the flesh. From the pounds the fish were gutted and transferred to the fish room where they were packed in ice. Care was needed here if the catch was to reach port in prime condition. After fishing, the deckhands had to swill all the surfaces down whilst on their way home. This led to a quick turnaround once the catch had been landed.

Obviously deep-sea fishing was no easy life, and where there is danger superstitions always appear and the fishermen have many taboos. No skipper will allow the decks of his trawler to be scrubbed until the journey home, although they can be swilled to keep them clean. No seaman will ever wear green or go to sea without a little money in his pocket – my father never allowed our family to wear green. Nobody was allowed to mention the word 'rabbit'. A friend of mine works in a pet shop in the town and one regular customer is a fisherman's wife whose children keep rabbits. She always asks for 'bunny mix' and not rabbit food. On American whaling ships of the 1850s it was also considered unlucky to use the word 'rabbit'.

Very few trawlermen, too, will mention the word 'pig' but prefer to say 'grunter' or 'curly tail'. It is probable that this superstition was brought to the Northern ports by men from Brixham who moved to be closer to the Arctic fishing grounds as steam replaced sail and the trawlers could reach these rich areas. The pig tradition seems to be more ancient than that of the rabbit, which animal was only brought to England by the Normans. Both pagan and early Christian mariners had a morbid fear of pigs. Perhaps it was because of the Old Testament reference to swine that hurled themselves, lemming-like, over a cliff and were drowned.

Another superstition is that wives can deliver their husbands to the docks but are never allowed to stay on and wave them goodbye. On no account will a fisherman's wife do a wash on the day of her man's departure. And any man whistling once aboard is given a very frosty reception.

The crew's payment is also of interest. Whilst the men were at sea the wives went to the owners' offices and collected a basic weekly wage, which they used to run the household. On the return journey the trawler usually docked in the evening before midnight and the crew would then go home. Between 6 am and 8 am the following morning the mate went down to the docks to supervise the unloading of the catch, which was done by land-based men called lumpers. The fish was then inspected and its quality assessed prior to an auction. The price obtained at this point was due in the main to the efficiency of the fish room workers whilst at sea. During the morning the cost of the catch was known and the crew's bonus calculated. At the conclusion of the sale the mate was issued with a summary of the transactions so that all knew that the crew were being treated fairly.

There are stories, however, of some owners doing a deal with the lumpers to hive off fish for themselves, some of which then left the ports for inland markets aboard what became known as the 'Ghost Train'. The lumpers may well have entered into deals as their work was hard, quite dangerous at times and the trawlermen called them the Midnight Millionaires. They had to take away the ice from the fish, pack them into wicker baskets and swing them up onto the quayside. The fishermen thought that some lumpers did not take enough care and the damaged fish did not bring the top price at auction.

Between 11 am and 12 noon the crew turned up for their 'settlings' plus their free parcel of fish. Many men then went on a spree around the pubs, but others returned home to their wives hopefully, but not always, with a fat pay packet.

What surprised me was how little time there was before the

trawler returned to sea; usually only one full day elapsed before they were on their way once more. A few men had some time off over Christmas and there was once a tradition of strapping a Christmas tree to the mast of trawlers; while sounding the foghorn was a New Year's Eve tradition which is now sadly, like the fishing fleet itself, almost a thing of the past. The length of time spent at sea varied according to the region fished and I discovered that four types of fishing vessel put out from the trawler ports, namely deep sea, middle water, near or North Sea and sea-netters or line fishers.

The deep sea trawlers fished the waters around Iceland, Norway, the White Sea, Bear Island and Greenland. Such trips were obviously of the longest duration and the main catches were of cod and haddock, both of which occur in huge shoals. They therefore provided the staple income of the trawlers, plus the more occasional solitary species such as halibut, sole or skate. These were very popular at the luxury end of the market. The deep sea vessels obviously carried the larger crews, and latterly they also had to employ a well-trained wireless operator whose presence must have made the men feel much less isolated.

The middle water trawlers, which were usually smaller, sailed to the Faroe Islands, the Shetlands and the waters just to the north of Scotland, and were seldom at sea for longer than a fortnight. They too caught haddock and cod but also a goodly number of dogfish, which were sold under the more attractive name of rock salmon. Dogfish belong to the shark family which are very primitive fish. The species present the fishermen with two particular problems. Sharks do not have skeletons of bone, but of cartilage and their skin is covered with very primitive tooth-like structures called placoids rather than the flat scales which cover the bodies of the more highly-developed bony fish. The deckhands gutting dogfish are likely to scrape their hands on these sharp placoids. Advanced fish also have swim bladders which fill with air and allow them to float in water without sinking. Sharks, including dogfish, have no swim bladder and thus they sink unless they keep swimming upwards which is most wasteful of energy. A netful of 'dogs' was therefore much heavier than a catch of cod or haddock with their swim bladders. All competent skippers are adamant that they could tell from the feel of their nets whether they had bony or cartilaginous fish within the mesh. There is a temperature gauge connected to the winch which hauls up the net and this always reads higher when 'dogs' are being landed. The fish can also be identified by an expert skipper by looking at his sounding apparatus.

Near water or North Sea trawlers were at sea for only around ten days and caught cod, haddock and flat fish. Like the middle water vessels, these trawlers could operate with slightly smaller crews and did not need to carry a wireless operator.

The fourth type of vessel was the sea-netter or liner which fished around Scotland and the North Sea as far as Denmark. The liners literally fished using baited hooks. Nobody must think, however, that work on a line vessel was for amateurs. The lines could be up to ten miles long and have more than 20,000 hooks laid out mechanically. These vessels have been adapted as gill-netters and beam trawlers. The gill nets were trawled behind the vessel and the fish were entangled by their gills.

None of the skippers I talked to objected to any of the above techniques and I never met a man who did not appreciate the need to conserve fish stocks. This is why, almost to a man, the old skippers worry about beam trawling which involves dragging chains over the bottom like a plough, followed by a wide net which catches the fish ripped off the sea bed. Caught in this way are Dover sole, plaice and other flat fish such as turbot. The seabed itself is damaged by this method, which disrupts the breeding grounds of the fish and also destroys the food chains of many other marine organisms. The reduction in the mesh size of the nets also catches smaller fish, many of which are not marketable except to grind up for animal feed or as fertiliser.

In the ever-increasing search for profit, pair trawling has also been developed. In a single vessel the net is trawled behind, with the size of the catch being determined by the area of the mouth of the net. With care a pair of skilfully manoeuvred trawlers can lay out a net between them thus considerably increasing the mouth size. When I first started talking to the skippers I assumed that the net was a simple bag made out of inexpensive string. How wrong I was. Each net is made by experts, costs thousands of pounds and is thus an item of capital equipment, the maintenance of which is a vital part of the work of a skilled deckhand.

Fishing techniques, including the design of vessels and catching equipment, are evolving all the time and their frightening efficiency is continually reducing fish stocks. Large vessels now spend months at sea and freeze their catch into huge blocks. Others use bright lights to attract fish which are then sucked up by a machine working like a powerful vacuum cleaner. It would seem that even the trawl net could eventually become a museum piece. Such drastic exploitation of fish stocks should clearly be discouraged or at least properly controlled.

Scientists must study the biology of each species and conservationists armed with facts should fight tooth and nail to preserve them. Human greed should never be allowed a free hand. In February 1992 the Japanese government agreed to discontinue the use of drift nets up to 40 miles long which caught squid and fish. They are known as 'walls of death' because they catch everything and not just specific species, and also kill many mammals and seabirds. Drift nets lost at sea remain operative for many years and can trap fish, mammals and birds for perhaps 20 years after the net is lost.

I spoke to Harry Chantler about this worrying aspect and he told me that all fishermen were like farmers and needed to have one eye on profits and one on conservation issues, and stressed the need to avoid greed from taking over. His whole life, he told me was devoted to fishing:

'All Fleetwood lads knew what they would do as soon as they left school – they would "go fishing". In 1955 I signed my indentures as a fishing boy and even then I knew that I wanted to be a skipper. I knew I had to work hard and do the job I was paid for. There were no short cuts. You had

The Boston Sea Foam *in 1958 and Harry Chantler, with cigarette, repairing nets at sea.*

to work through all the stages. After a year as a fishing boy I first became a half deckhand, then a three-quarter deckhand and after 18 months I was a fully fledged deckhand and knew all about the roughness of the sea. At 17 I became a bosun and then the real hard graft started. You had to have four years' time out at sea. They were very strict on this and every day you were out there was counted and added up.

'Once this four years were up you could sit for your mate's certificate. Aboard a trawler the mate was in charge of everything beneath the bridge. The mate was responsible for everybody and answered only to the skipper who really was the "god above". The only way a skipper was judged was by how much fish he brought back. The owners worked on this principle and, as the crew were paid a percentage of the catch, the men wanted to sail with the best skipper. There was a saying that a skipper was only as good as his last trip. I worked hard and was a skipper by the time I was 23. There is no doubt that luck comes into it and all skippers kept a steady eye on the weather. The best conditions for fishing the Arctic waters was a force 4 or 5 which did make the trawler

Harry Chantler and the tie up of the cod end.

wobble a bit. Flat calm was a problem because we needed the motion to keep the nets away from the side to avoid crushing and damaging the fish in the mesh.

'Skippers, bosuns and mates learned to pick out the good deckhands and made efforts to keep them on board for their next trip. A good trawler crew was made up of a team from skipper to fishing boy. We soon learned to recognise and get rid of drunks who were no good as trawlermen and were actually a real danger in a situation where each man had to rely on his shipmate.

'Any vessel fishing in the high Arctic all the year round had to face hazards which those reading these words will find hard to imagine. Icing was one real hazard because the extra weight festooned on the rigging could create lots of weight and cause the vessel to capsize. The ice had to be chipped off by hand and axes were used but great care was needed to ensure that the rigging was not damaged. We used things like wooden mallets or baseball bats.

'Catching the fish was one thing but storing it and keeping it in good condition was another and a good fish room team was worth its weight in gold – literally. First the fish was gutted which was a very difficult job in freezing conditions. I've known fish freeze as they were being gutted. They were then washed and the flesh sent down into the fish room, sorted and packed in ice. The deck was then washed and all the guts flushed out much to the delight of the birds. The nets were examined, repaired if necessary and out went the trawls again as quickly as possible. You could feel the elation of the whole crew when they saw a net bulging with valuable fish. There was many a glance up to the bridge if the catch was a poor one!

'Once a skipper decided that it was time for home then there was a time to relax – almost, but not quite. I did all my training in Iago vessels so there was some degree of comfort but it was still cramped, often wet and always cold. No skipper would allow his trawler to enter harbour looking

Lumpers at work.

anything other than shipshape and the day before landing, decks were scrubbed, paintwork touched up and brasses polished. Once the ship was berthed the crew left and the catch was taken over by the foreman lumper although the mate was allowed to check the catch figures. On leaving, each man was allowed to take home a feed of fish and they were often given another feed along with their wages. Some lumpers, but by no means all, were honest and some had all sorts of pockets fitted into their oilskins. The fish in these cases was often sold to men in vans who then drove off to the Lancashire mill towns. Many of these workers did indeed earn large "lump" sums. As soon as possible the fish were auctioned off and the money obtained was calculated and recorded in the owners' offices. The men then turned up to be paid. Skippers and mates were paid on a percentage basis as well as a daily rate whilst at sea. The deckhands had a weekly wage which they could rely on plus a small percentage of the catch.

A fish auction in full swing.

'Any vessel tied up at her berth was a financial liability and so the turn around had to be fast. The basic idea was to land the catch on Friday morning and be out at sea again on Sunday. We all wanted to keep making money, especially if we had not had a successful trip. Fishing went on over Christmas and the New Year. There were occasions when an experienced mate wanting to become a skipper could take the ship to sea and give the skipper the festive period at home. All skippers had their favourite areas to fish and had the incentive to be good navigators. They were also good fish biologists. They knew which fish were found at their best in each season and so varied their fishing grounds accordingly. Even when I buy fish today I think about the best time of year to eat it.

'One final and most important thing that I soon learned as a skipper is to rely on a good crew. If you looked after them and brought home good catches they looked after you. A reliable crew was worth its weight in gold.'

One man who worked all his life as a deckhand was Mick Rodgers who told me:

'You can always tell a trawlerman by looking at his hands

Mick Rodgers – A life at sea as a deckhand.

and by watching him walk. Most of the long-time deckhands like me have arthritis in every joint.

'I left school at 15 in 1963 and began working for the Boston Deep Sea Company as a ship's painter. I soon realised that lads going out to sea on the trawlers were earning more money than me so I signed up when I was 16. I began as a galley boy and I've never been so ill in my life. There's nowt worst than sea sickness. Imagine a high sea running and I'm sat there peeling spuds and putting them into ice cold water. Suddenly the metal bucket lurched across the deck and I waited for the next roll to bring it back because I were too ill to move. It was then I realised how a good crew worked together. A deckhand looked at me and told me to go and lie down and he continued with my work.

'The galley was cramped and the crew liked chips and boiled spuds. What a danger that was with a sea running. We had pans with lids which could be tightly sealed but we still had to hang on and not get burned by the hot pans and gas. Despite this I still enjoyed it and was surprised at how much trawlermen like eating fish. To a galley boy it was our idea of heaven if we were travelling on a calmish sea and we could peel our spuds out on the deck.

'I'd been at sea for nearly two years on the *Wyre Majestic* when the skipper Alec Middleton came up to me and asked whether I was ready to go out on deck. I worked my way to three-quarters deckie and then a full hand. There was lots to learn such as mending nets and gutting fish. This is no problem in decent weather but we didn't get much of that in the freezing waters we were out in.

'When I started, the duty roster was 18 hours on deck and six hours off but sometimes you did not get that and I can remember on some occasions being too tired to eat. A doctor from Grimsby did a stint on a trawler and suggested that a minimum of six hours exclusive of meal breaks should be allowed and the Board of Trade agreed. Meals were important and I knew from my time as a galley boy that to the crew the most important man aboard was the cook.

'Breakfast was to start at 6 am and half an hour was allowed. Dinner was at noon and was also to take half an hour. Tea was between 6 and 7 pm and could last one hour. Obviously storage of food was an important feature; it was space rather than temperature because the ship was a floating refrigerator. This was solved by the crew eating lots of fish – sometimes as often as twice a day.

'Apart from the sheer hard work of being on deck, one

Peeling potatoes on deck.

member of the crew had to watch from the bridge and keep an eye out for a big wave coming. He would then shout a warning and those on deck grabbed hold of something solid to avoid being washed overboard. It was a great feeling coming home with a full load of fish knowing that a decent pay day was coming. We needed a good sleep after landing and then to go to the owner's offices to collect the pay.'

There was often an excellent relationship between the owners, the skippers and the crew and apart from pay there was only one bone of contention. This was a tradition which some owners – but not all – tried to suppress and that was the practice called 'pleasuring'. This involved a father taking his son out on a trip during the school holiday. The idea was that as sons followed fathers into the job it was as well for them to get used to life at sea. This was certainly going on in Fleetwood during the 1960s.

It is therefore not surprising to find family groups with as many as four generations enjoying a chat and being able to describe the transition of trawlers from the days of steam to the cleaner days of diesel-powered ships. The womenfolk were in full agreement with this pleasuring process because they knew of nothing else and they themselves were often working in the supporting industries which abounded in the fishing ports.

Chapter 6

The Support Industries

When people talk about the decline of the fishing industry in Fleetwood, they naturally think of the trawlers rusting away. When I spoke to Harry Chantler, Dick Gillingham and Mick Rodgers, and especially to David Pearce who in the 1960s was the Dock Correspondent and later Editor of the *Fleetwood Chronicle*, they all made the point:

'For every man that went to sea there were at least ten other men and women who worked either at home or in factories connected with the industry. There were lumpers, filleters, auctioneers, barrel and box makers, braiders and networkers, painters and rope makers, firms making winches, cranes and other items of ship and dockside "furniture", along with painters, welders, maintenance workers, riveters and a host of small businessmen who had their own fish vans which they drove to the Lancashire towns. Although in a limited way, the open air markets at places such as Clitheroe and the Lancashire mill towns still have a space for the Fleetwood fish van man to sell his wares, which varies according to the catch available.'

Dick Gillingham told me:

'If you want to understand how much of Fleetwood once depended upon fishing, you must visit the site of the Asda store. Many of the support complexes were here. There is the Goth Funnel Memorial outside the store; I was asked to design the panel associated with the funnel at the request of Asda and via the Fleetwood Civic Society. Where you now do your shopping was once the main trawler offices and the Great Grimsby Coal, Salt and Tanning Company, the Fleetwood Trawlers Supply which was a massive chandler's, and also the Fleetwood Vessel Owners' Association Offices.'

However busy Asda gets on a peak shopping day, the crush could not be compared with the one-time ants' nest of a complex which was the nerve centre for the whole Fleetwood fleet. Apart from works producing salt and a myriad of processing works, many fishermen's wives worked at home. Many were netmakers called braiders and they could suspend the nets they were making from doorframes and look after the children at the same time. They were supplied with raw materials at their door and the completed work was collected and paid for.

Ethel Chantler was a braider whilst her husband was away at sea and she told me:

'Braiding was a family business where daughter followed mother. It was often done at home with the net being hung on the backs of doors. My mother worked at this until she was over 70. I learned from her and I was able to thread needles from the time I was eight.

'Braiding needles were not a bit like sewing needles. These were flat wooden structures about ten inches long

Braiders at work.

and about one inch across. The needle was held in the right hand. The rough twine was looped inside the needle onto a device called a lug and pulled tight with your left hand. This made your hands very rough and sore and to make them tougher they were soaked in methylated spirits or, if times were hard, in urine. To keep a good braider going you might need as many as six needle fillers. This meant all the young lasses learned to do this from an early age. All braiding was done by piecework and the net companies brought the twine and collected the finished bits of net. We loved it when we were given the cod end of the net because it was more intricate and you got paid more for it.

'Unmarried girls were often employed in braiding works. I worked at Gourocks by the dock gates. Piecework certainly kept you hard at it. The bits of nets we braided were then taken to the net makers who were called riggers. As you can imagine, these nets were huge and when they were being made they were hung from high roofs. I loved the smell in the works because the nets were soaked in tar so that they would not be destroyed by seawater. You could always tell a rigger because he had black hands. Braiding was a happy job because you knew that if you had been good at your job you would be able to work from home when you married and had children to look after.'

A hardworking trawler fleet was also supported by fish filleters, curers and smokers, shipbuilding and especially repair workers and there were those making clothing and footwear – the list was almost endless.

Leather hand-crafted sea boots were expensive but so well made that they could last the whole of a man's working life and even then they would have some secondhand value. Clog makers also did a roaring trade in the fishing ports where the alder and beech soles stood up well to the wet and slippery conditions encountered by lumpers, filleters, barrow boys and those who did brisk business at the fish auctions.

The merchants' warehouses which were so much part of Fleetwood, especially when the deep freeze facilities evolved, were very much a feature of fishing ports. Some of these buildings still survive in Fleetwood and can be seen on a drive into the town.

There were also a number of bonded warehouses where skippers could order the alcohol and cigarettes which were to be taken out to sea and not therefore liable to tax. Harry Chantler told me:

'This buying of booze and fags was a very necessary chore because some but not all fishermen were hard drinkers. Skippers soon blacklisted the men who came aboard drunk, secreted booze in their packs and were a hazard on board. We all liked a smoke but we had to be safe and a drunk could threaten the whole ship. A skipper bought from a bonded warehouse out of his own pocket and doled the goods out to the crew. A few skippers made a profit but most of us played the game and just covered our costs. When we fished we liked a bit of movement to keep the nets away from the side. A flat calm was no good for hauling nets. With the sea moving in anything above a force 4 or 5 the last thing you want is a drunk lurching about. Once blacklisted, news got around and a man had to prove himself to be more reliable in future if he was to get another job. To navigate properly a skipper needed reliable men while he got some sleep and only stone cold sober men could be relied upon.'

The fisherfolk in all ports, including Fleetwood, have long memories and some speak of the Depression of the 1930s as if it was just yesterday. Around Lancashire and in Fleetwood especially in terms of this book, the lack of work created great hardship. It is in this context that when a fleet of fifteen Unilever trawlers sailed into the Wyre Dock a right royal welcome awaited what was called 'The Northern Fleet'. Flags flew, whistles blew, bands boomed and the mayors of Blackpool and Fleetwood shook hands with everybody, children cheered and the *Fleetwood Chronicle* waxed lyrical about a 'Fishing Boom, Pioneers of a New Adventure' and reported at length the speeches made at civic receptions.

Alas, this laudable dream turned into a nightmare as a year later in 1937 Unilever sold all of its fifteen trawlers, which then sailed away to ply their more lucrative trade out of Grimsby.

Nobody likes war but in retrospect when the Second World War broke out in 1939 it gave people a reliable job for the first time in more than a decade. Trawlers out of Fleetwood which had been struggling to make a living were requisitioned by the Admiralty and many trawlermen set out not just to battle with the sea and the shoals of fish but to face the enemy with its smaller but much more lethal shoal of U-boats. The fishermen were useful to the Admiralty in another way. They knew of safe landing places around the Arctic and could advise with regard to where U-boat bases would possibly be located, especially around Bear Island.

It is interesting to note that in the 1930s the Germans were carrying out what they called 'vital experiments on weather forecasting' and had several Arctic weather stations. The trawlermen knew where they were, and signed the Official Secrets Act to work with the Admiralty to provide vitally important information which may well have played a major role in the eventual victory at sea in the Atlantic.

What is not often known is that the trawler crews got to know the people who lived in these remote islands, such as St Kilda, as I discovered when I sailed as the resident naturalist on a converted trawler taking visitors to these areas in the 1980s. I also once had the pleasure of interviewing Margaret Shaw-Campbell, the wife of the Laird of Canna, who in the 1920s had made her name as a photographer of scenes of the Outer Hebrides. She asked me to take some of her photographs with me and to photograph the same scenes some 70 years on. This was to be a Then and Now record.

Margaret told me:

'You've been out to St Kilda and you know how rough the sea can be even on the calmest of days. The people found it impossible at times to keep in touch with their many relatives who had emigrated to the mainland and to such far-flung places as the USA and Australia. The people would write letters, often in Gaelic, and place them in bottles in the hope that some kind soul would post them on. From the 1890s there were regular visits from Fleetwood trawlers and they passed on mail. There was the occasional landing and goods were carried using an accepted barter system. I was there when some of these exchanges took place and also on one occasion witnessed a landing. When St Kilda was finally abandoned by its people in 1930 the Fleetwood link was broken but even when I visited the Hebrides the descendants of the St Kildans still talk of the 'Fleetwood ships', even though their island home is now a distant memory.'

'Unloading' goods on St Kilda.

Mick Rodgers recalled:

'Oh aye, we all knew St Kilda long after the people had left in 1930 and we used it as our last landfall before heading out to the deep seas. I have met lots of the St Kildans' descendants now living on the mainland and they still tell tales of their visits from the "Fleetwood fellas". The crews bought warm ganzies, which were thick pullovers made from the wool of the Soay sheep which still live on the island but they are now wild. The Fleetwood fellas did not pay cash but bartered with fish and especially salt which the islanders used to preserve some of the birds which they caught such as gannets, puffins and guillemots.'

It was around the stormy waters of St Kilda that a Fleetwood trawler hit the news when one of the great stories of seamanship made the headlines in the 1920s. The *Hayburn Wyke* hit a huge

For pleasure not work – a trawler returns to the Hebrides.

wave and her rudder was destroyed. The vessel was owned by the Dinas Steam Fishing Company, an offshoot of the Marr family. Her skipper, J.W. Green, proved to be a seaman of high calibre. He took the otter boards of the fishing net and made a makeshift rudder. They lay the vessel on the sheltered side of St Kilda and improvised a new rudder. To do this they flooded part of the trawler which raised the rudder area. Three brave crew members including the bosun, Jess Summer, and two crewmen, Smith and Harrison, risked life and limb to stabilise the new rudder. They then made the 300-mile journey and were given a heroes' welcome back in Fleetwood.

There are still no permanent residents on St Kilda but the old stone cottages are now restored and rented out to visitors by the National Trust for Scotland. That is providing they can get out there, because the sea is often too rough to land.

In both world wars the Germans were aware that St Kilda had a

*A trawler's otter-door jury rudder: photograph taken on arrival home
after a 300-mile passage from St Kilda.*

radio link and therefore provided an advanced warning of enemy movements. They actually shelled St Kilda in the First World War and were no doubt aware of what was going on in the 1940s.

In both wars, too, trawlers were pressed into service. Even my limited experience of sailing in these waters showed me just how seaworthy the vessels were, but they certainly gave the crews a rough ride on occasions.

Chapter 7

Trawlers at War

In the context of this book there are not two but three wars to consider: the two World Wars and also the Cod War. In terms of damage done to the fishing industry the Cod War was by far the most devastating, largely because the British government did nothing to help our own trawler fleet. In fact, it could be argued that successive British governments have done their best to cripple their own trawlermen. It is hard to blame the fisherfolk for being so bitter. To be honest I agree with them.

In both the first and second world wars the Admiralty requisitioned trawlers to serve as escort vessels and especially as minesweepers. They also 'called up' the skippers and crews. Being part of the Royal Navy the vessels had to be 'captained' by a serving officer. These were usually youngsters with little if any experience at sea and everybody on board knew who was in charge and that was the trawler skipper. This hierarchy was almost always accepted by all, even when the vessel came under attack. Trawlermen of experience never seem to understand the word 'panic'!

The Marr trawler Maretta *did her stint as a minesweeper during the war.*

Most trawlermen and their families still had the events of the first war etched in their memories when the vessels were requisitioned as minesweepers in the Second World War. In 1939 the naval signal announced that 'Winnie is Back' and as Churchill became Lord of the Admiralty they were poised for action. This did not take long as the Prime Minister-in-waiting set up his 'Utmost Fish' directive. This resulted in the establishment of the Royal Naval Patrol Service using trawlers often crewed by these carefully selected fishermen. Many men were posted to Lowestoft, where they became affectionately known as Harry Tate's Navy. Their base was close to the Sparrow's Nest theatre complex.

One Fleetwood vessel was the *Osta*, a trawler which saw service in both wars, but at the same time new 'trawler type' minesweepers were being built. One such was the *Sir Garaint*, a Round Table class naval trawler which was launched in 1941.

Minesweeping was very costly in terms of ships and the lives of

Names of the men who died while serving in the RNPS.

brave men. By the end of 1940 over 100 Royal Naval Patrol Service vessels had been lost; at the end of hostilities there were 2,000 ships and 70,000 men in service. In the Fleetwood Museum there is a room devoted to the service and rightly and proudly displayed is a memorial to the men who lost their lives.

Some minesweeping trawlers were kept in service well into the late 1940s as 'stray' mines were a real problem when old fishing and shipping lanes were opened up as trade picked up at the end of hostilities.

There were Fleetwood trawlers in the thick of the action at Dunkirk and supporting the Normandy landings, as well as keeping the Arctic Convoy routes swept clear of mines. Shipyards in the town were busy 'degaussing' trawlers: the engineering works of James Robertson based in Dock Street were skilled in constructing rings of special material around the wooden hull of the trawlers so that they did not set off the clever fuses designed

A trawler on escort duty (left), under depth-charge attack.

by the Germans to detonate the mine when it came in contact with metal immersed in sea water and which generated a small electric current. Robertson's also devised equipment such as winches and depth charge throwers which operated without producing a spark.

Another important development used on trawlers was the latest design in radio communication. Just before she died at the age of 96 in 2008, I met with May Davies, whose husband Neville had served in the Navy during the war. He had written down his memories:

'I had always wanted to go to sea and at the age of 15 I joined a whaling fleet and became a radio operator. As war approached I was forced into the Royal Navy as a Radio Operator officer. In 1940 I was attached to the crew of a Fleetwood trawler. This was converted into an escort vessel and a minesweeper. There was a Naval officer in charge but he was young and the ship was really run by the trawler skipper. His men looked up to him and when we were pushing through rough seas or being subjected to

H. Neville Davies, naval radio officer, 1940.

enemy action I never saw one man take a backward step. The only time they complained is that to start with they were not given any weapons to "have a go back". I remember seeing a Grimsby trawler being attacked on a freezing morning in January 1940. There were lots of injuries on the *Rigoletto* and the skipper and the mate were both killed. These trawler lads were the toughest and friendliest bunch in the world and during the war they forgot all about the inter-port rivalry and got on with the job. They learned to hate the Germans and loved their English ale and spirits.'

The war was not easy for the trawlermen because like the rest of the Merchant Navy there was no pay if you were not at sea and you were not at sea the second the vessel you were sailing in was sunk! In the first three months of the war Fleetwood's fleet lost

The Rigoletto.

seven vessels and this meant that 37 men and their dependents were left penniless. This applied even at Dunkirk when trawlers were pressed into service to ferry troops from the beaches, often under very heavy fire.

Arthur Lewis, the skipper of the Fleetwood steam trawler *Evelyn Rose*, returned from a fishing trip very late one Saturday night and by Sunday morning his catch was unloaded. He was then given secret orders to set out to sea to Plymouth, to join with a very junior officer who, as we have seen, was only present as a gesture. His White Ensign flag was replaced by the red banner of the Royal Navy and the trawler headed for Dunkirk. There under heavy fire she took on board 317 sailors and ferried them to Ramsgate. Off she went again to the beaches and took off another 400 British and French soldiers.

Mick Rodgers remembers talking to some of the Fleetwood men who were at Dunkirk and he smiled as he told me:

'Most obviously objected to being shot at during the war but what annoyed them more was that they were not able to fire back. Eventually some trawlers were fitted with guns and the lads went to Liverpool to be trained on how to use them. This made them feel better. Us trawlermen live a tough life and are used to fighting the sea and sometimes each other in the pub if things get hectic. To a single man they all wanted to have a go at "Jerry".'

It was not just the *Evelyn Rose* which braved the beaches of Dunkirk; other Fleetwood trawlers involved were the *Velia*, *Dhoon* and *Jacinta*. Arthur Day was skipper of the *Gava*, by that time a member of the Naval Patrol Service, and had a particularly rough time – and that is saying something. Three of his crew were decorated for their bravery in rescuing some wounded French soldiers in the face of German Stukas dive-bombing the area. These brave lads deserve to be remembered and they were James Jones, Harry Gwanne Ganne and Arthur Dunne.

Obviously, because of the importance of food, some trawlers had to be employed catching fish but these were often the oldest and slowest vessels. Because Hull and Grimsby on the east coast were closest to the European theatre of war most of the trawlers were based out of Fleetwood, which became the major fishing port for the duration. At this time the Fleetwood fleet was joined by fishermen who, often with their families, had fled from the Germans by running the gauntlet of the Nazi patrols.

One such fisherman, Otto Jensen, was a crewman aboard the Danish vessel *Vestland* which was only built in 1937 and was the largest seine netter in Denmark with an overall length of 85 feet. Otto recalled:

'We escaped on 7th April 1940 and sold our catch in Grimsby. We were then taken into custody to make sure that we were not German spies. Once they realised we were Danish we were taken to Fleetwood and soon found jobs on trawlers and learned the language – usually swear

The Fleetwood crew of a trawler at war, complete with dog mascot.

words first – quickly. All of us English and Danish had a common language which we called Fishing and a common enemy which was the German aircraft, gunboats and U-boats.'

All the trawlermen knew of the dangers and two Marr vessels, the *Lord Minto* and *Artha*, were sunk by gunfire from a U-boat whilst they were fishing off the Flannan islands late in 1939. Hitler had given orders that no prisoners were to be taken and that crews were to be shot. The fewer men there were fishing the less fish would be landed in the ports. Some, but thankfully by no means all of the German U-boat captains, obeyed this command! The Dunkirk evacuation and the D-Day invasion in the opposite direction were high profile events even though the trawlers are usually given far too brief a mention, but one aspect of the war receives hardly a glance. This was the ill-fated Narvik operation in Norway. The aim here was to prevent the rich iron-ore mines in this area from falling into German hands but the British troops were not properly equipped and a withdrawal was essential. Fourteen trawlers under the banner of the Royal Naval Patrol Service were lost in the operation and many Fleetwood men were part of this sacrifice. In total 13,890 men from the service lost their lives and this represents a mortality rate of one in six! All these men were officially classed as civilians which is an obvious disgrace even when looked back at over a period of around 70 years.

These events and those who lived through them are fading into history as time takes its toll. But there was one war which still causes anger – even more anger than the German conflict – and this was the so-called 'Cod War'.

The trawlermen and their families fully understood the perils of war. What they did not – and still do not – understand is why in the third war which brought defeat they were totally without the support of their own successive British governments.

Whilst life was always hard for trawlermen they were reasonably secure and therefore happy until 1976 when what became known as the Cod War with Iceland was fought and lost by Britain's politicians who had, according to the fishermen, more on their minds than fishing. As the British trawlers became more and more efficient, the Icelanders, quite rightly, became worried that the fish breeding stocks were under threat and also that their own trawlers were being crowded out by larger foreign vessels. As the Icelanders used up the stocks of fish inside the twelve-mile limit they decided to move out but the British were already fishing there. The Icelanders therefore proposed to increase their territorial waters from twelve to 200 miles, a massive increase. Most British fishermen agreed that some extension was necessary and would initially have probably accepted a 30- or even 50-mile limit but 200 miles was far too sweeping. They also felt that it was

British expertise which had mapped and opened up the fishing grounds and the Icelanders had picked up many secrets from a study of the ships whilst in harbour for minor repairs or seeking shelter from adverse weather. In retrospect, the British trawlermen were very badly treated.

As the Icelanders were bilingual they could also listen in to radio conversations whilst speaking to each other in their native tongue which the British could not understand. Around 1976 the mutual mistrust which had been brewing for a number of years was brought to a head by the Icelandic Communist party, who proposed the removal of American Navy bases and the Western fishing industry, either of which would have been good news to the Russians. Few wars were colder than this one played out in Arctic waters. Many fishermen believe that diplomatic pressure was applied by the Americans to persuade Britain to accept the 200-mile fishing limit because they feared that otherwise their military bases could be closed and thereby create a vacuum which would soon be filled by the Soviets.

Whatever the political truths may be, there is no disputing that the British government was under immense pressure. They had to satisfy their American allies on the one hand and public opinion on the other, which was very much on the side of the fishermen. God help the politician who threatens the British fish and chips either then or now! The scene was set for conflict and the poor old trawlermen were firmly in the middle. The trawlers tried to continue fishing within the 200-mile limit and were given some, but little more than token, protection by the few British warships which were present. The Icelandic gunboats tried to cut the trawl wires knowing that a lost and expensive net meant that the fishing trip would almost certainly run at a loss.

The war was not without its moments of black humour as reported in the *Daily Express* of 3rd February 1976:

'*Flying the Flag – New Flare-up as Cod War Skipper Hoists Skull and Crossbones.* Today trouble began when the Icelandic gunboats *Tyr* and *Aegir* harassed a pack of

30 British trawlers for three hours. The *Tyr*'s captain told the trawler skippers to stop fishing and haul in their gear. They all stopped, except the *Ross Khartoum* from Grimsby. Skipper Derek Keetley hauled up the skull and crossbones and, still fishing, sailed towards the gunboat. The Icelanders say the *Tyr* appealed to Mr Keetley three times to take in his gear and leave. When he refused, the gunboat eluded the two watchdog trawlers guarding the *Khartoum* and cut the trawler's warps. The Whitehall version of the incident is that the skipper was in the middle of hauling in his nets when they were cut. The incident happened 40 miles off Iceland's south-east coast. An official of the British Trawler Federation said later, "It shows our skippers still have a good sense of humour – though it was not appreciated by the gunboat captain".'

Newspaper reports are not always famous for their accuracy, especially when trying to hit deadlines. I have it on the best authority that the crew of the Grimsby trawler did not fly the skull and crossbones until three days after the event and there were no watchdog trawlers operating although skippers did keep in touch.

Looked at in the cold light of historical day the British fishing industry did not decline but was quite deliberately and cynically betrayed by our own politicians because of their own selfish ambitions. From 2002 onwards papers released under the 30-year rule prove beyond doubt that fishing – one of Britain's major industries – was sacrificed by politicians and proved that European leaders also played their own underhand game. Let us look carefully and critically at the facts.

In 1973 Edward Heath was determined to take Britain into Europe and was prepared to go to any lengths to see that this happened. Papers recently released from their secret listing in 1971 clearly reveal the deep level of duplicity. Furthermore, ministers were prepared to back the Prime Minister to further their own careers.

In June 1970 Britain, Ireland, Denmark and Norway had been

about to apply for membership of the Common Market and the six original members were aware that these four countries together would control 90% of Europe's fishing grounds. The scheming six laid their own clever mesh to entrap what they saw as the favoured four. They proposed that all fishing grounds should be shared by all countries. This was never anticipated by the Treaty of Rome but Edward Heath was told that if he closed his eyes to this change in policy then entry to the Market would not be blocked. Civil servants and Opposition MPs including Harold Wilson pushed for a House of Commons vote but this did not happen. The result was that France was allowed to control 90% of all the cod caught in the English Channel. The original twelve-mile limit was then extended to 200 miles – once again without a Parliamentary vote and Britain's fishing fleet was consequently reduced whilst those of France and Spain were dramatically increased.

Fleetwood skippers, as well as those operating out of Grimsby and Hull, were rightly incensed at what one skipper told me was 'A Treaty of Treachery'.

It seemed that the situation could not get worse but it did and again British politicians did nothing to help their own fishermen. The so-call Cod War revealed even more treachery. 'No trawler man will ever trust a bloody politician,' was repeated to me time and time again as I gathered material for this book, *Memories of the Lancashire Fishing Industry*. One trawler owner said to me,

'What about volume two – call it "In Memoriam of Lancashire's Fishing". I'm not "codding", it really does need to be highlighted. It's true so why don't you write it as it was.'

No historian should ever tamper with the facts and now the documents of the time are open to public scrutiny there can be no doubt that the British fishing industry was betrayed and those who were employed in it have every right to feel bitter.

By the mid-1980s there were no distant-water boats operating from Fleetwood and the Boston Deep Sea Fisheries Company was no more. Hundreds of men who had known nothing but trawling all their working lives were thrown on what is best described as the scrapheap along with their rusting vessels.

David Pearce, who was the Dock Correspondent of the *Fleetwood Gazette*, told me that for a while Fleetwood trawlers made a good if short-lived living from providing support vessels to the developing oil rig platforms. Later, however, the oil companies had their own purpose-built vessels and the life of trawlers was over.

The Marrs did not lie down and die but searched for new markets as their vessels had wider and wider ranges. In 1982 five of their vessels were requisitioned and saw service in the Falklands War. The five vessels which functioned successfully as minesweepers were *Cordella*, *Farnella*, *Junella*, *Northella* and *Pict*. They were captained by Royal Navy men. Once again we see British governments taking much from the trawlermen but giving nothing back in return. Those who face the danger of the sea deserve a better deal from politicians sitting comfortably at their desks. They can get sacked – but perhaps not enough of them – but they will never understand what it is to be shipwrecked.

Chapter 8

For Those in Peril

In the 1940s I spent my childhood in the village of Askam-in-Furness on the Duddon estuary and we all knew the fishermen. The Constables ran a grocer's shop and what they did not sell was not worth having. Gibson Constable ran the shop and his father went fishing. Gibson had one counter scrubbed white and either full of fish or waiting for the catch to come in. I remember waiting in a queue for the fish to arrive by cart along Duddon Road and Gibson saying to a group of us children, 'My dad's my boss and his boss is the sea. You lads who go aht wi' thee fathers should never forget that.'

One of my friends did not heed this warning and went out on his own to fish and a sudden storm came up and wrecked his little boat. Alan's body was found six weeks later washed up on a sandbank. The biggest bunch of flowers I have ever seen at a graveside came from Gibson Constable.

Even the most experienced trawlerman would echo the words of Gibson Constable – none more so than Harry Chantler and his wife Ethel. During the course of many conversations I have had

The fishing boat Peggy LR9 *was pounded to pieces in less than ten minutes alongside Kilnbrow slipway, 12th January 1962.*

with this couple Harry said,

'I was one of the lucky ones. I did get wrecked on my very first trip as a skipper and I thought my number was up for sure.'

Ethel then said,

'I knew what was happening before he came home and we both knew how close I was to losing him. Some Fleetwood families were not so lucky and I never pass the fisherman's memorial without a mixture of joy at still having Harry and sorrow, and I do shed a tear for my friends who lost loved ones.'

Harry went on to tell me,

'Do you know what my prized possession is and I've always kept it? It was a letter from the Mayor of

Fleetwood telling me that he was pleased that me and all my crew survived to tell the tale. I'll tell you another thing which all fishermen here would agree with after a really rough trip – that was the joy at seeing the two lighthouses guarding the entrance to the harbour. There was nothing like it, but we all had a living to earn and were eager to challenge the sea again. Some of the old-timers tell of the three lights which first operated in 1840 and which lasted until 1948 when one was destroyed by fire. One thing you must do, Ron, and that is to record the lives of those who died at sea and were not able to set down their memories.'

It was here that Joyce Openshaw, a former director of the Iago Company, lent me a copy of a book called *Fleetwood's Fishing Industry* which dealt with deep-sea vessels between 1840 and 1990. Peter Horsley had a photographic business in Fleetwood and from the early 1950s his camera was never still, whilst co-author Alan Hirst retired to Fleetwood in 1962 after a career as a schoolmaster in Rochdale. These two have compiled a fitting memorial to those who went fishing for the last time and never came home alive. These sad events date from 1880 to 1976; I have traced 76 vessels which were wrecked with the loss of at least 354 lives.

Joyce Openshaw remembers the wrecking of *ST Red Falcon* off Skerrymore in 1959 when 19 men were lost:

'This was the worst day in the history of the Iago Company and we were all devastated. What can you say to a grieving woman with children at her skirts? We lost a ship but the families lost loved ones which is much more important.'

There is not one person who has survived a shipwreck who will not constantly remember the experience and revere the memory of those who were not so lucky. One man who survived not one but two shipwrecks was the retired deckhand Mick Rodgers, who told me:

'It has to be said that nobody in their right mind likes to be shipwrecked but it's almost worth it to enjoy the feeling of relief when you are rescued. In the course of my trawling days which began in the 1950s I was shipwrecked twice.

'The first time was in the *Boston Lightning* and I remember the day because we were listening to a radio commentary, it was when Henry Cooper knocked Cassius Clay down and the count went on and on so that Cassius could recover and Henry lost. It was blowing a gale when we were struck amidships by the Grimsby trawler *Lord Howe*. Her bow was embedded in our vessel but the Grimsby skipper kept his head. We were losing water but the *Lord Howe* partly sealed the gap. We were able to launch a boat and then board the *Lord Howe*. The Grimsby lads then went astern and took us to a safe billet on the west coast of Iceland.

'The luckiest man alive that day was Jimmy Crisp who was our wireless operator. He had just left his radio room when the collision occurred and a Grimsby anchor demolished his radio room completely.

'By that time the sea had slackened and the *Boston Lightning* did not sink. The skipper, mate and chief engineer went back aboard and eventually she was towed back to Fleetwood for a major refit. I have to say that the owners and insurance company treated us well and we were flown back home and given new clothes and put on survival pay for a month.

'My second shipwreck involved the *Wyre Conqueror* and as we set off to Iceland we were having radar and compass problems. We ran aground on Portland Lowshore which is on the east coast of Iceland. What seems to have happened is that the vessel had been fishing in near waters and in this case iron bobbins to weight the nets were used because we did not need to use sophisticated electronics. When deep-sea fishing was the route, then the iron bobbins were replaced by heavy wooden blocks. In this case the exchange was not made.

'We were rescued by a Hull trawler, the *Hull City*, but our skipper, his mate, the chief engineer and the cook stayed on board. This was just before the cod war and an Icelandic gunboat called the *Odin* took on a tow and we were taken to a small port where the Icelanders entertained us in some style. The insurance people again turned up trumps and we were given new clothes and a macintosh of high quality.

'Clothes given to shipwrecked men included a new suit and all that went with it. We were flown home and I remember this flight because on it was the film star Britt Ekland. Again we were given a month's survival pay but then you had to find another ship but nobody worried because fishing was our lives and we loved it and knew nowt else.'

The crew of one vessel which was not so lucky was the *Evelyn Rose*, which was wrecked on New Year's Eve 1954 off Ardtornish Point around Lochaline in the Hebrides. Twelve of her fourteen crew were lost, only Ernest Meyer and William Crawford survived. Richard Barton was the chief engineer and his son has spent many years tracing the fate of his father's ship. 'Young Dick', now in his sixties, told me:

'I was seven years old when my father was lost and I was his only child. I remember the event clearly. It was on New Year's Day 1954 when I was wanting to watch a television programme called *The Grove Family* at 7.30. Suddenly the family all came around and I was packed off to bed without watching the programme. My mother was crying and I never knew why. Next morning my mother woke me and told me that my dad had been lost at sea. His trawler had foundered on rocks and dad had gone below to collect life jackets. She sank and then slipped down into a trough and was lost. They say that children have no lasting memory but this is not true. My mother did, I think, die of grief at the age of 50 and for my whole life I have wanted

The Evelyn Rose *in her prime, 1946.*

to have my father buried properly but this had never been possible until February 2008.'

Dick met Mark Lawrence who runs the Lockaline Diving Centre on the peninsula and he located the wreck of the *Evelyn Rose*. That it was her was confirmed by Steve Brown, a diver who filmed a DVD of the vessel. Dick Barton takes up the story as I spoke to him in September 2009. Between us we looked at the DVD and Dick pointed out:

'You can see the gallows, which is the apparatus used to hoist the fishing nets, and also you can see details of the wheelhouse. A dive is now planned to remove an item or two from the trawler and bring them to Fleetwood Museum to be used as a focus for the *Evelyn Rose* to be properly commemorated. I now want to bring my father's remains home so that he can at last rest in peace.'

The *Evelyn Rose* herself saw action during the Second World War and she helped in the evacuation at Dunkirk. She berthed alongside a flaming pier and took off 403 troops. She was so badly damaged that she had to be beached at Ramsgate. She was repaired and returned to fishing after the war but in 1948 she sprang a leak off Iceland and managed to limp home to Fleetwood. In 1949 she hit rocks around the Western Isles but was successfully salvaged and none of her crew was injured. This was typical of many trawlers and not many people realise just how hazardous these fishing waters can be. The last word on this tragic event has to be with Dick Barton Junior:

'I know that it is not possible for people reading this account to realise just how Fleetwood folk like me feel at a loss such as this. I still sit quietly by the memorial on the promenade and still wish I had a father to have shared my life. I was at school with Dick Gillingham who designed the memorial and he knows how this loss affected me.'

The memorial is situated between the small lighthouse and the Knott End Ferry and the Lifeboat (RNLI) Base and Information

The memorial to the Fleetwood fishing community.

Centre. This latter building serves as a reminder of the brave men who risked their own lives in an effort to save others. Once again I found that there are lots of living memories of the lifeboat days over the years.

I got into the heart and soul of this tradition when I visited Barbara Woodhouse at the Lancaster Maritime Museum, where she has worked for some 30 years. She told me:

'Both my father and grandfather were members of the Morecambe Lifeboat crew which operated from 1895 to 1987. It all began on 3rd September 1894 when a Morecambe pleasure boat called *Matchless* hit a sudden storm near Grange-over-Sands with the loss of 25 people. The local fishermen, including my grandfather, were convinced that Morecambe needed a lifeboat and approached the Royal National Lifeboat Institution but they said that another vessel was not needed as there were stations at Fleetwood and Barrow on each side of the Bay and a Morecambe boat would not be necessary. The reaction of the Morecambe men was one of anger and they set about raising the money to launch a boat. They knew that when the tides around the town were accompanied by sudden gales it would need prompt attention if boats caught in these conditions were to be saved.'

In 1893 the local fishermen had formed a Fishermen's Association, which was already well organised and ideally placed to build one extra vessel for the express purpose of search and rescue. A tragic event known as the Blackpool Gale on 2nd October 1895 resulted in the essential funds for a lifeboat being raised very quickly.

Following a beautiful 'Indian Summer' a huge gale blew up without warning when 18 boats from Fleetwood and 15 from Morecambe were trawling for shrimps. These sail-powered boats had no chance. Many were blown ashore on the Blackpool sands but six fishermen were lost. From 1895 until 1987 the

Morecambe lifeboat operated successfully and saved many lives. Barbara Woodhouse's family had connections with the Morecambe lifeboat for the whole of its existence. She takes up the story from first-hand experience:

'To begin with, the first lifeboat was bought secondhand and was an 18-ft long salmon fishing boat which had operated on the River Lune and had a beam of 6 feet 6 inches. She had an almost flat bottom which meant that she could operate in shallow water. An agreement was made with the owners of the Central Pier to erect two boarding platforms and with metal ladders leading down from the pier. The *Gyakhan* had sails but also two rowing positions on each side of the boat. It was known from the onset that the *Gyakhan* was too small but was a stop-gap and Crossfields Boatyard at Arnside was commissioned to build a purpose-built lifeboat. The *Rescue* was 24-foot long, had a beam of 8 feet and had buoyancy tanks which meant that she could right herself if she capsized. She was launched in 1907 and my grandfather was there.'

The fishermen's second lifeboat Rescue *heading in towards Green Street landing stage during a crew exercise, August 1926.*

The *Rescue* certainly earned her name and did sterling service and saved many people. There were never less than two of the Woodhouse family in the crew and the Willacy family were also prominent. In 2005 Keith Willacy printed privately a comprehensive history of this lifeboat service. By the late 1920s the *Rescue* was fast approaching her 'sell-by date' and once again the RNLI were approached to provide a boat. Their reply was the same as in 1895 – the stations at Barrow and Fleetwood were adequate despite the *Rescue*'s record of saving life.

When I spoke to Barbara Woodhouse in September 2009, she said:

'I still remember my father saying in later years that he was angry at this refusal and did not see that there was a future for a Morecambe Lifeboat. Then came a lifeline due to the fact that so many people from West Yorkshire were spending their holidays in Morecambe and it was known as Bradford-by-the Sea. Lady Priestley, the widow of a wealthy Bradford industrialist, agreed to fund the building of a purpose-built lifeboat providing that it was named after her husband. Crossfields of Arnside was commissioned and the *Sir William Priestley* was launched in April 1934. She did sterling service until 1987 and my father was coxswain for many years. In the war she worked ferrying crews to and from the oil tankers which were berthed at Heysham Harbour. These were huge to us at the time but minnows compared to the monsters which we see today. In 1958 I remember my father working with the police to experiment on installing reliable portable radio communications to link shore and sea. I have a photograph of this experiment. Another thing that I remember is the excitement the family felt when a black bakelite telephone was installed in our cottage which enabled us to be contacted by the coastguards and police instead of them having to run and knock on the door. My father then had to rush round, knock up his crew and head out into the teeth of a gale.'

Lady Priestley performing the naming ceremony of the fishermen's lifeboat, named after her late husband Sir William Priestley who had been a Bradford industrialist.

By 1987 the RNLI had an efficient Inshore Rescue network and as the relations between this body and the Morecambe Lifeboat were very cordial it was decided to retire the *Sir William Priestley*. She is now in the Lancaster Maritime Museum awaiting what will be an expensive restoration.

It is not within the brief of this present work to spend much time on the RNLI operations within the boundaries of old Lancashire except to point out that local fishing families still form part of the crews as they have more seawater in their blood than most of us. No chance should be missed to visit the RNLI bases at Lytham St Anne's, Fleetwood and Barrow.

This wonderful voluntary service deals with coastal waters but those who fish in distant waters know only too well the fatalities

The Sir William Priestley *tries out a police portable radio in an attempt to establish the practicality of installing a radio in the boat, summer 1958.*

The Sir William Priestley *returning to her mooring after attending to the fishing boat* Wahine LR44, *12th January 1962.*

which can be caused by an often angry, relentless and unforgiving sea. As long as there are fish in the sea and the men willing and able to catch them these perils will remain. The fisher folk of Fleetwood today still face this danger but sadly they also have other problems to face. These problems will, I am sure, be met head on but life, as well as the sea, is likely to be rough in the future.

Chapter 9

Full Circle

Long before the time that Fleetwood was being planned and built from the 1840s onwards, fishing families were moving to the area from often very tiny villages all around the Lancashire coast. There are families like the Leadbetters described earlier, who were there from the beginning. Ethel Chantler, whose maiden name, as we have seen, was Leadbetter, told me:

> 'I can't remember a time when fishing was not part of my life. My family fished mainly just off-shore. Folk drank their tea and talked of the latest developments. They remembered sail being replaced by coal and steam, then came diesel which allowed the boats to travel even further and faster.'

The new equipment allowed more accurate navigation and there was also fish-finding sonar which could identify shoals and even indicate species.

For many years the diesel-powered side trawlers – called sidewinders – became the mainstay of the industry until the coming of the 'stern trawlers'. Stern trawlers were certainly more efficient than the sidewinders and obviously involved a new design of trawler. Also called stern draggers, Fleetwood's first

Local fishing continues on the Lancashire coast as it has done for centuries.

stern trawler was the *Criscilla*. She was a Marr vessel and the largest in Fleetwood – 952 gross tons. Her design was revolutionary as she was built to a specification allowing her to get through the narrow locks at Fleetwood and to be compatible with the port's crane system which allowed for easier unloading.

The sidewinders had their main superstructure amidships and running aft. This allowed the foredeck to be open for the crew to work on but they were exposed to the full force of the elements. On stern fishers the low foredeck was built up with accommodation forward. The net was shot aft and when emptied it was into a chute over the stern and into the fish deck where cleaning and gutting was more easily carried out. The offal was discharged by chute over the side.

These trawlers had high bulwarks which offered more shelter than was the case with the sidewinders, where losses of men overboard were regarded as an occupational hazard. It must be agreed that the stern trawlers arrived too late as the 1970s saw a decline in the trade, which affected Fleetwood more than other ports.

Ethel Chantler lived through this decline and told me:

'The memories of the trawler fleet need to be written down and your book will help. The best thing I ever did was to start work at Fleetwood Museum. It keeps me in touch with the fisherfolk who keep dropping in for a brew on the boil and a chat. You just need to sit here with a brew always kept on and they will drop in and talk to you.'

This proved to be great advice and all I had to do was to keep my notebook and pen handy and wait for invaluable information to arrive. I got to know Mick Rodgers really well and he told me:

'When I first started trawling as a lad in the 1950s, conditions were appalling but in the space of about ten years things changed. Obviously, fishing in cold waters is never easy but if you are waterproof, have a cosy bunk and are well fed things ain't so bad.

'At first you had to provide your own clothing and as we were poor to start with we were not well equipped for fishing among the ice. I well remember the joy when we were provided with free clothing – it really were like a pay rise. We were given two choices. You could have a "frock", which was an all-in-one weatherproof piece of kit with a hood, a pair of thigh boots and twelve pairs of gloves, or you could have what was called a "duck suit". This was a jacket with a hood and a pair of waterproof trousers which came up to your waist. For this you were given half boots and the usual twelve pairs of gloves which you really did need.

'You were also given bedding allowances which included a mattress but only one blanket. With us on the *Boston Phantom* there was Bill

The radio room of the Jacinta.

Brookes, whose father was a tailor. Bill used to bring offcuts of no use to his dad and he stitched these up to make warm clothes for the crew to wear under their waterproofs and he even made extra blankets. These underclothes were called "doppers" and everybody wanted to go trawling with Dopper Bill Brookes.'

Everybody who works hard and in cold weather needs lots of food and this was true in trawlers. Some skippers who had enjoyed a profitable trip would entertain their crews before the next sailing and provide them with plenty of food and drink. Good cooks were worth their weight in gold, and Mick Rodgers never failed to mention just how important this was.

'In my lifetime at sea the food improved as the trawlers got bigger and were designed better but apart from fish the staple diet was "duff". Before things got better I remember one chief engineer actually stopped the ship and when the skipper asked him what the problem was he growled, "Some bugger's pinched my bloody egg".

'Duff was almost like a huge dumpling and the cook had to make it soft so that it soaked up the gravy or the custard. On one occasion the duff set so hard that one of the crew took it ashore and it was used for years as a doorstop in a Fleetwood pub.

'We were never short of cheese because in them days it were cheap and good cooks baked their own bread. They would leave out hot loaves for crews coming off duty and with lots of butter, corned beef and sometimes an onion and it were a treat. All the milk was tinned and you could also bring your own along, with tins of Horlicks or Ovaltine. When the weather was fairly calm it was not the best time to fish but it did give the cook a chance to provide us with lots of chips. It goes without saying that the best fish and chips in the whole world were aboard a trawler with a good cook.'

Harry Chantler, who was a trawler skipper out of Fleetwood from the 1950s, agreed with Mick Rodgers:

'I already told you that a sensible skipper made sure to keep reliable crew members but it was vital to have a good engineer to keep the trawler machinery happy. It was just as important to have a good cook to keep the innards of the men happy.'

Good cooks in all walks of life need good fish to make their diners happy and it is already becoming far too evident that over-fishing without concern for conservation is a disaster waiting to happen and it is now a case of not 'if' but 'when' fish stocks decline. Politicians all over the world will have to tackle this problem head on and not dodge the issue. What will always go on around the Lancashire coast, though perhaps to a lesser degree than in former times, is estuary and near-water fishing and, of course, cockling and shrimping.

The history of the Lancashire fishing industry has now come full circle and it is still revolving, although much more slowly these days. So long as there is fish to be caught and enjoyed there will be fisherfolk. They will prove to be the best farmers of the shallow sea if only big business and politicians let them get on with it. We do need to go back to our ancient roots which are still there, if not always realised.

Those who read these words should realise that this is living and ongoing history. Why not use the last chapter of this book as a tourist guide and visit the villages which are still full of fisherfolk and also the museums which are staffed by folk with their families steeped in this aspect of maritime history? And don't forget to buy the fresh fish and shellfish on offer and enjoy the scent and, especially, the taste of the sea.

Chapter 10

Places to Visit

Those who wish to celebrate the Lancashire fishing industry will not only want to read books but also to visit places where they can talk to people who were a part of this history. Museums are manned by volunteers with fishing in their blood and visitors should not be afraid to ask questions – the volunteers love it when this happens. The museums should not be rushed and the modest entry fees are well worth the money.

The *Jacinta*

The *Jacinta* (pronounced 'Jashinta') is moored in the fish dock, and Fleetwood – now not crowded with trawlers but a huge marina – is doing brisk business associated with the expanding tourist trade. Access is via a signed walk through the Freeport Village where there is plenty of free parking.

The *Jacinta* is open between Easter and the end of October from 10 am to 3.30 pm, but at other times by appointment (telephone: 01253 885642). The vessel can be hired for functions and will include catering, with Lancashire hotpot being a speciality! School parties are welcome and will be told that on a fishing trip the *Jacinta* could bring home enough fish to produce 3.5 million fish fingers. Does any child want a second helping?

The *Jacinta* is no ordinary trawler but was once the top of the

The Jacinta.

range. It was built for J. Marr and Son at Wallsend in 1972. In 1975 she became the record-breaking vessel for a Fleetwood wet fish catch when she landed 188 tons following a 19-day trip around the Icelandic fishing grounds. In 1982 Marrs had to switch their operations to Hull and in 1986 she became Britain's top earning trawler when the value of her catch was £1.3 million. In 1991 she broke another record when she landed 230 tons of fish which sold for £270,516. In 1994 she was the top-earning British trawler, with her yearly catch being £1.94 million, and this was over only a ten-month year as she was being serviced for two months.

The *Jacinta* was therefore a world-beater and the envy of all others. She is a 615-ton stern trawler and took a crew of 16. She is 50 metres long, 9.75 metres wide and needs 6 metres of water to float in, with a powerful 1900 horsepower engine, and travels at 11 nautical miles per hour. This gleaming vessel is no museum piece but can go to sea, and takes part in Naval Reviews. I was shown a photograph of the *Jacinta* sailing beneath the Clifton suspension bridge near Bristol and it is not stretching the truth too far to say that two wonders of British engineering were in this photograph at the same time.

I was lucky to climb aboard the *Jacinta* to meet Lionel Marr whose company built the vessel and who, along with the Trust and volunteers, has been responsible for her restoration. The yellow superstructure was a feature of all the Marr trawlers. I enjoyed a cup of tea whilst gasping at the number of photographs showing trawlers at work, some of which have been used to illustrate several chapters in this book.

Lionel then took me on a tour of the ship. Looked at from the harbourside she seems small but distance can, as always, be deceptive. The only way to describe the interior of this vessel is to make a direct comparison with Dr Who's Tardis.

I was taken firstly into the fish hold, which used to hold 2,300 tons and part of which has been converted into a museum and exhibition centre. Here events are held such as carol concerts for as many as 120 people. Events can be planned and christenings on board have been one feature of the variety of themes on offer.

Part of the fish hold has been restored to show its original function and is divided into metal cages called pounds. Here the fish were packed in ice and close by is the fish factory area. The fish from the nets was pushed down into chutes where they were gutted. This had to be done because the bacteria in the gut would have caused the fish to rot despite the efficient icing process. Part of the Fleetwood back-up services were ice factories where the essential substance was produced. One of these factories is still in use and provides ice for the catering services of restaurants and supermarkets.

The guts from the fish were pushed through small chutes and into the sea much to the delight of the birds, especially gulls, which waited eagerly for the scraps. One piece of the gut which was not discarded was the liver and these were placed in a huge drum. This produces cod liver oil. It is sold on landing but the sale went directly to the crew as a financial perk.

From the fish room I was taken up to the bridge which is now gleaming and restored to look as if it had just left the maker's yard. The modern trawler skipper not only has to be a first rate seaman and navigator but also something of an electronic whiz kid. He has to understand radar and echo-sounding equipment which is so sophisticated that it cannot just pick out the dangers lurking on the seabed but also shoals of fish. A skilled operator can also work out the species of fish he is looking at on the screen. The *Jacinta* skipper must have been very skilled indeed judging by the number of records which she shattered.

Close to the bridge I saw the tiny wireless room, which must have been a godsend because the vessel could be in almost constant contact with home. Crews of the *Jacinta* were well catered for in terms of comfort compared to the old days. Even the

Jacinta *on her way back to Fleetwood from Northern Ireland in May 2009. The bronze statue on the Esplanade is called 'Welcome Home' and commemorates the lives of Fleetwood's fishermen and their families.*

gutting was not carried out on the open deck but in the drier area of the fish factory and the bunks for the off-duty crew were warm and dry. When I was shown the galley, I was reminded of a well run hotel kitchen except that the plates and cooking utensils were secured in racks. As I toured the vessel she was standing still. The *Jacinta* at sea was a different kettle of fish altogether as she had to ride some of the fiercest of the Arctic storms. During days of rough weather the crew had to be fed and no trawlerman had an easy day. He was hard at work all day and needed lots of calories to keep him working. I tried to think of what the *Jacinta* must have been like at sea and Lionel Marr did his best to get this across to me but unless one has actually made the voyage it is not possible to realise just how hard life was.

Visitors to the *Jacinta* should take their time and talk to the guides, who are all ex-trawlermen, but above all they should remember that this vessel, given 48 hours' notice, could be ready for sea.

The Asda Supermarket, Fleetwood

As described in chapter 6, on the site presently occupied by this supermarket, there once stood a complex of fishing company offices on Dock Street and leading up to the Fleetwood Arms pub which still stands. In the Asda car park there are murals relating to the heyday of the trawlers designed by Dick Gillingham, and also the funnel of the *Goth* which once sailed out of Fleetwood.

The supermarket is on the outskirts of the town centre and close to the entrance of the Freeport Retail Outlet. This has been developed on part of the old Fish Docks and near to the developing marina complex.

Dick Gillingham gave me a photograph of the Dock Street complex, in which the flag is at half mast, obviously relating to a trawlerman's loss. The buildings themselves from left to right are Fleetwood Trawlers Supply, Boston Deep Sea Fisheries, J. Marr and Sons Limited, the Great Grimsby Coal, Salt and Tanning Company, Armours and the Fleetwood Fishing Vessel Association. There was once a glass canopy over the pavement

Dock Street, now the site of an Asda supermarket.

outside the Coal, Salt and Tanning Company. Men looking for a ship gathered here and were said locally to be 'under the coal salt'.

Fleetwood Museum, Queen's Terrace

Fleetwood's maritime heritage collections are held at Fleetwood Museum (telephone: 01253 876621) and the museum has been operating since the early 1970s. The original local history collection was displayed in the former reading room of Dock Street Library (previously known as the Fielden Library and Whitworth Institute). In 1982 the collection was enlarged and allocated more space as part of the Maritime England Year. The collections were moved into the former reference library and two basement rooms, and Lancashire County Museum Service took over the management of the museum. In 1992 the museum and its collection moved into one of the town's most historic buildings, the 1838 Custom House designed by the eminent neo-classical architect, Decimus Burton. Over the years, the building has been used as a private residence, a school, council offices and Fleetwood Town Hall.

Fleetwood Museum.

The museum is listed as a Grade II building and is set in a designated conservation area, consisting of the early buildings and layout of the new town of Fleetwood. It occupies a splendid location overlooking the River Wyre. From the first floor windows visitors can experience the maritime panorama of the river, of Morecambe Bay and across to the beautiful Lakeland hills.

Amongst the prized exhibits are the two historic fishing vessels, *Harriet* and *Judy*. *Harriet*, built in Fleetwood in 1893, is one of the few wooden-hulled fishing smacks in existence and is listed on the National Register of Historic Vessels. The museum is attempting to have the *Judy* listed too as she is a fine example of a Morecambe Bay prawner. *Harriet* can be viewed but by tour on certain days only, with experienced guides who bring her fascinating past to life.

Within the main museum building, visitors can find a warm welcome in the newly constructed Coffee House, an ideal spot for a break following a museum tour or shopping in Fleetwood's famous traditional market, just a two minute walk around the corner. The Coffee House features a magnificent stained-glass window, originally in Fleetwood Grammar School and designed by Ann Howarth in 1964. The museum shop displays a wide range of quality gifts and books, with an emphasis on the maritime theme.

Many of the galleries in the museum have a maritime flavour, with areas devoted to Fleetwood Port, Deep Sea Fishing, Inshore Fishing, the Royal Navy Patrol Services and the Royal National Lifeboat Institution. An interactive Netting The Bay computer gallery allows visitors to embark upon a (computer-based) voyage out to sea.

In December 1959, the trawler *Red Falcon* was lost with all hands near Skerryvore in Western Scotland. Fifty years later in December 2009, hundreds of visitors arrived to commemorate the tragic loss at a seafront Remembrance Service, organised by the museum and the Royal National Mission for Deep Sea Fishermen. Many visited the museum also to view the superb scale model of the *Red Falcon*, and the related archives, news stories and photographs on display in the Deep Sea Gallery. Superb scale models of Fleetwood-based fishing vessels alongside huge and heavy items of fishing equipment, are eye-catching features here.

In the adjoining Port Gallery, a huge scale model of the Port of Fleetwood in the 1930s clearly shows the importance of the railways, as Fleetwood grew to become the UK's third largest fishing port. Long before deep sea fishing became the town's staple industry, the port did for a time compete with Liverpool for a share of the cargo trade. Huge four-masted barques came round Cape Horn with cargos of grain, etc., from the USA and other far flung places – fascinating paintings bring this period of maritime history to life.

In the Inshore Fishing Gallery, cross the boardwalk above the sands of Morecambe Bay, to view the traditional methods used by Victorian and Edwardian fishermen in their search for cockles, mussels, prawns and shrimps. Alongside in the Royal Naval Patrol Service Gallery, the heroic stories of Fleetwood trawlermen engaged in minesweeping duties during the World Wars are brought to life.

Children find the recreated Salt Mine particularly exciting, most likely because it is dark and slightly spooky. Across the River Wyre, the Preesall Salt Field provided the raw material used by a major chemical industry, ICI, upriver at Thornton.

Children make up a large proportion of visitors to the museum, with school parties arriving from all over Lancashire. Particularly popular is the Victorian themed fortnight in May, with its working demonstrations of steam power and a live Punch and Judy show. During the rest of the year, children can experience the charms of the Victorian Boarding House and Dining Room. They are able to handle numerous Victorian household objects and even dress up as Victorian children! During the school holidays, the museum hosts lively Arts & Craft sessions for families, always well attended and often fully booked. It also hosts a popular afternoon series of local history talks during the summer months.

The museum is close to Fleetwood's unique main street tramway, dating back to 1898. The system is currently being redeveloped to allow continental-style supertrams to bring visitors from Blackpool.

The town of Fleetwood is due to celebrate its 175th birthday in 2011 (the first house in the town was built in 1836) and a special exhibition is to be staged to celebrate the event. The museum is at the heart of Decimus Burton's Fleetwood – a unique set of classically designed buildings by the famous architect. The majestic Queen's Terrace and the elegant curve of the North Euston Hotel are just a stroll away.

Huge container ships ply their trade from the Ro-Ro berth opposite to the museum building and you can also see the Fleetwood to Knott End ferry operating across the Wyre, as has been done since the 1840s.

Fleetwood Museum actually closed in 2006, but many local people rallied round to persuade Lancashire County Council to continue supporting the town's museum. At present, Lancashire County Council, Fleetwood Museum Trust, the Friends of Fleetwood Museum and over 50 wonderful volunteers work alongside staff to keep the unique visitor attraction open. The museum has served the town well for nearly 30 years and hopefully can continue to do so for many years to come.

Lancaster Maritime Museum

This excellent museum is housed in the 18th-century Customs House designed by a member of the Gillow family, famous for its furniture (telephone: 01524 382266). The exhibits include a detailed history of the inshore fisheries based around Morecambe Bay and many of the staff are from old fishing families. Here are to be found old lifeboats, fishing vessels and a boiler once used to

The Lancaster Maritime Museum.

cook the shrimps, which were then potted in butter. There is a café and a good book shop and excellent disabled facilities, plus lots of informative leaflets. The Friends of the Museum do a wonderful job in helping to keep the exhibits in good condition and there is an extensive archive which is made available to interested parties, including school parties, students and authors.

There are exhibits devoted to shipbuilding, which was also once important in the area, whilst the modern industry based upon the oil exploration and distribution along the north-west coastline is graphically explained.

To get to the museum from the town centre, follow the signs for the Maritime Museum which is located at St George's Quay where there is limited street parking restricted to two hours but there is other parking further on.

Apart from the above-mentioned places, many of the historic fishing villages on the Lancashire coast featured in this book are still largely undeveloped and well worth visiting.

Index

126

Also by Countryside Books

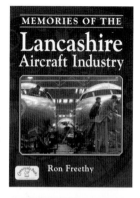

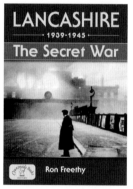

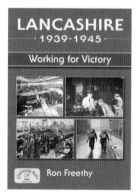

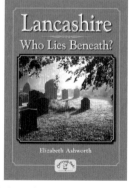

www.countrysidebooks.co.uk